Proverbs
Idioms
and Expressions

A Guide for Interpreters and Translators

To Douglas,
a very special and good
student who helps to
make the class fun

Con todo cariño

Leonor

by
Leonor Valderrama de Sillers

Ilustración de cubierta (Cover Illustration) por
Eva Moreno de Valderrama

Library of Congress
TXU1-190-143

ISBN 0-9762403-0-0

ACKNOWLEDGMENT

To my mother, Eva Moreno de Valderrama, who always has
a saying or proverb appropriate to every situation. When I
was growing up in Colombia I never dreamed that what I was
learning from her then would be so valuable to my career as an
interpreter and translator.
Gracias, Mijita.

All my love and appreciation to my husband Douglas, to my
sons Steven and Joshua, their wives Julie and Sarah and to
my granddaughter Erin for their special knowledge, which
contributed to this dictionary.

AGRADECIMIENTO

A mijita, Eva Moreno de Valderrama, quien siempre tenía
un dicho o un proverbio para cada ocasión. Nunca pensé que
lo que estaba aprendiendo en mi casa en Colombia un día
me sería tan útil en mi carrera como traductora e intérprete.
Gracias mijita.

Todo mi amor y agradecimiento a mi esposo, Douglas, a mis
hijos Steven y Joshua, a sus esposas Julie y Sarah y a mi nieta
Erin por el conocimiento tan particular que han aportado a
este diccionario.

TABLE OF CONTENTS

GUIDE TO USING THIS DICTIONARY

This dictionary has been organized in alphabetical order according to the first word in the phrase. From my experience as a court interpreter, I know that this dictionary will assist interpreters to be more accurate and more efficient. The speed at which an interpreter needs to interpret vocabulary, expressions and legal terms into the Target Language does not allow much time to look through a large and complicated dictionary. When searching for a term, the interpreter needs to look for the letter of the alphabet under which the term has been cataloged. If, on the other hand, it is necessary to research proverbs, idioms and expressions by "key word", the interpreter must find where that word is in the dictionary. For example, with the proverb, *Put your faith in God and keep your powder dry,* the first impulse of an interpreter would be to look for the proverb under the key word **God**. The list of entries for the word **God**, however, is very extensive and the expression may not even be there. The interpreter may then look for it under the words **faith, powder, dry,** or the verb **to put.** All of this would take a considerable amount of time that the interpreter does not have when there may be six or more people waiting for the interpretation. In the manner that I have organized this dictionary, the interpreter would only need to look under the letter **P** for the word **Put**, which is the beginning word of the proverb.

A blank space has been left after the meaning of each proverb, idiom and expression. The space after the English to Spanish portion is intended for interpreters of another language (i.e.; Somali, Arabic, etc.) to write the saying in their language for future reference, (See attachment A). The blank space after the Spanish to English portion is intended for a Spanish interpreter to write another variation of the same proverb, idiom, or expression, in Spanish, (See attachment B). The reason that there may be another variation is related to the cultural differences and some differences in language usage that exist among Spanish speaking countries. For example, the English expression, *You cannot make an omelet without breaking some eggs,* in Colombia y becomes: *El que no arriesga un huevo no tiene uno pollo* (One must risk some eggs in order to have chickens). In Spain, the same idea is expressed as *Quien no se arriesga no pasa la mar (One can not cross the sea without taking some risks).* The meaning is the same. The context from which the images are drawn is different.

In both the Spanish and English sections the proverbs, idioms and expressions appear in bold print in their language of origin, followed by the equivalent in *italics*. The definition of the original proverb, idiom or expression is immediately below in normal type.

Attachment A

Arabic

- **A bird in the hand is worth two in the bush** – *Más vale pájaro en mano que ciento volando.*
  This saying advises us to take advantage of what we have even if it is less, or smaller, than what we might hope to get if we bypass what we have for sure.

  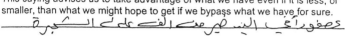

Bosnian

- **A bird in the hand is worth two in the bush** – *Más vale pájaro en mano que ciento volando.*
  This saying advises us to take advantage of what we have even if it is less, or smaller, than what we might hope to get if we bypass what we have for sure.

  Bolje vrabac u ruci nego ptica na grani

Somali

- **A bird in the hand is worth two in the bush** – *Más vale pájaro en mano que ciento volando.*
  This saying advises us to take advantage of what we have even if it is less, or smaller, than what we might hope to get if we bypass what we have for sure.

  Miro gacmaha kugu jira, miro geed saaran looma daadsho.

Attachment B

Spanish

- **De grano en grano llena la gallina el buche** – *Many a nickle makes a muckle.*
  Every little bit helps.
  Se usa para indicar que mediante el ahorro módico pero tenaz se alcanza la riqueza. También se usa para dar a entender que con paciencia y de a poco se pueden alcanzar grandes cosas.

  Grano a grano, hinche la gallina el papo.

INTRODUCTION

As I was growing up in Colombia, I was always aware of the numerous proverbs and sayings that were incorporated into our daily lives. It seemed like older people, in particular, spoke in proverbs all the time. My mother's day would begin with, *A quien madruga Dios le ayuda* (The early bird gets the worm), which was her way of exhorting my sister and me to get up and start the day. *El que quiere celeste que le cueste* (Nothing ventured, nothing gained), was her answer every time we wanted something, but complained about the difficulty in obtaining it. In addition, we could never complain about a gift we had received, as she always replied, *A caballo regalado no se le mira el colmillo* (Never look a gift horse in the mouth). She had a proverb for every daily event and so did many others. We lived in a "sea" of proverbs. At school, for example, the nuns would impart their wisdom with sayings that they felt would enhance our scholastic, cultural and religious education. Admonishing us to be quiet, they would say, *En boca cerrada no entra mosca* (Silence is golden), or *El que mucho habla, mucho yerra* (The less said, the better). We were encouraged not to be idle with, *El tiempo perdido los Santos lo lloran (Time is golden).* These sayings made up a great deal of everyday speech. They were so prevalent that I didn't think of many of them as specific expressions, but rather as just a natural part of communication.

When I came to the United States and began to learn English, I realized that there was a universal component to sayings and proverbs. *Don't put the cart before the horse,* for example, has its Spanish counterpart in, *No ensillar antes de traer las bestias. Más vale pájaro en mano que ciento volando,* translates into English as, *A bird in the hand is worth two in the bush;* and *El que con lobos anda a aullar aprende* is, *If you lie down with*

v

dogs, you get up with fleas. In both Spanish and English, the proverbs use the same basic reference, but they are adapted to fit the rhythm, rhyme and alliteration of the particular language.

When I entered the profession of court interpretation, I became more aware of the prevalence of proverbs used to express a wide range of concepts.

I heard attorneys make comments like, *Birds of a feather flock together;* and *Where there is smoke there is fire.* On the other hand, Spanish speaking clients said things like, *El que no llora no mama* (The squeaky wheel gets the grease) and, *A lo hecho, pecho (It is no use crying over spilt milk).* This added to the already difficult task of accurate interpretation. I learned very quickly, how critical it was for me to become familiar with a number of, proverbs, idioms and expressions, in both languages. I also recognized that a reference book of proverbs, idioms and expressions would be very helpful for interpreters. It was at that time that I decided to research this area and to develop this reference guide.

As a starting point for my research I began the with premise that, "In order to render a complete an accurate version of the SL message, the interpreter must conserve every single element of information that was contained in the original source language (SL) message," (González, Vásquez and Mikkelson, 476). This is, in fact, required by the "Code of Professional Responsibility for Court Interpreters". When dealing with proverbs, idioms and expressions, the difficulty of this obligation to completeness and accuracy is compounded by the language and culturally specific metaphors that are the essence of many proverbs, idioms and expressions. This makes it all but impossible to transfer them, in verbatim form, from the Source Language (the language from which one is interpreting), into the Target Language (the language into which one is interpreting).

Semantic Foundation

There are certain aspects of languages that are universal, such as the fact that most languages are based on sound. All are structured to communicate the speaker's point of view and the words themselves are organized in a way that expresses their meaning. The learning of words is not the learning of a language. While words are definitely a part of a language, it is their combination with other words, in grammatical structure and "shades of meaning", that convey ideas. However, proverbs, idioms and expressions, are lexical units that can not be modified by changing a word. By doing so, the meaning can be lost. For example, the saying, *A bird in the hand is worth two in the bush* won't have the same meaning and effect if we change it to, *A bird in captivity is worth two in the bush.* Others are based on plays on words, the case of the Spanish expression *Salir de Guatemala para entrar en guatepeor.* It doesn't have any thing to do with the country of Guatemala or the word *guatepeor*, which is not a valid word, however, it has to do with the endings *mala* and *peor* (bad to worse), (Azevedo 264). In this sense, proverbs, idioms and expressions, are as much a part of a language as are the individual words and structures. María Leonisa Casado Conde in "Se dice pronto" says, "Dominar una lengua implica no solo manejar con habilidad los mecanismos de funcionamiento de la misma, sino también conocer el hecho diferencial, las variantes de índole cultural que conforman una determinada realidad." (Command of a language implies not only the skillful handling of its mechanics, but also knowing the differences in meaning, the cultural and sociological variations that agree with a given reality.) (9).

Because the human experience is similar the world over, and because languages and cultures have always borrowed from one another, many proverbs, idioms and expressions have equivalents in several languages. It is essential for the interpreter to "build a store house of equivalents"

(245), upon which he or she can call instantly. For example, upon hearing the English expression " *You are between a rock and a hard place,*" the interpreter should react instantly to convert the phrase into its Spanish equivalent: *Está entre la espada y la pared* (You are between the sword and the wall). Although it sounds poetic, this form is not a familiar saying in English and would be an incorrect interpretation. At the same time, there are proverbs, idioms and expressions which do not have a true equivalent in the target language because they have developed in a culturally, or geographically, isolated way and are specific only to the context in which they were created. The Spanish proverb, *Tanto va el cántaro al agua que por fin se rompe,* (The jug goes after water so often that it finally breaks) from Don Qixote, has no real equivalent in English. In order to maintain the obligation to completeness and accuracy, therefore, the interpreter must be able to express a similar concept concisely, without entering into an explanation and, in this case, it would best to choose the English expression, *Don't press your luck.*

A proverb, as Luis Alberto Acuña says, "Tuvo por padre al pueblo, por madre a la experiencia... amigo es de todos, pero muy particularmente de los viejos..." (Had the people as a father and experience as a mother...is a friend of all but especially of the old folks.) (9-10).

Sources

Proverbs come to us from innumerable sources. Many have their origins in the agricultural life of times past when animals, weather and crops dominated everyday life. *Entre ecuestre y pedestre* (He doesn't know if he is afoot or on horseback), for example, was used when people traveled by horse. Over time, this expression has come to signify someone who is confused, or doesn't know what to do. Others have their origins in religion. The "Sermon on the Mount" in the Book of Matthew, includes the teachings of Jesus that have become proverbs. One of the more familiar proverbs in the Sermon is, *Judge not that ye be not judged.* They are still popular sayings and proverbs today, even though some have been slightly changed over the years. In his "Dictionary of 1000 Proverbs, "Peter Mertvago also points out that there are Arabic, Roman and Christian influences in Spanish proverbs and sayings (8). This, he says, may be due to their collection by monks in the Middle Ages and their use in the moral education of youth.

Proverbs, idioms and expressions change with time, like everything else. They evolve, develop and mutate to fit the context in which they are used. In "La Celestina" by Fernando Rojas, the proverb *Da Dios hauas a quien no tiene quixadas* changed to *Dios le da pan a quien no tiene dientes* (Life isn't fair), the idea is the same, however, the words have changed. The words *hauas* and *quixadas* (beans and jaws) have changed to *pan* and *dientes* (bread and teeth). With the passage of time, the aspects of a language change. There are changes in pronunciation, meaning and use of words. New words come into a language and old ones disappear. Due to these changes, new metaphors, which are more apt to the times, are also created (Azevedo 16). *You can't make a silk purse out of a sow's ear,* had literal currency in a by gone time when most people knew what a sow was and understood the difference between the smoothness of silk and the rough texture of this part of the pig. Today, even though it enjoys frequent use, many repeat this proverb without any notion of the meaning of this reference. A more modern proverb from the 1950's is attributed to plainspoken President Harry Truman who said, when speaking of being able to put up with stress and pressure, *"If you can't stand the heat, get out of the kitchen."* The uncomfortable nature of the hot kitchen is not in itself a modern reference, as hot kitchens have existed for centuries. To apply, however, the metaphor of a hot kitchen to the very contemporary context of pressure and stress creates a present day proverb. The Colombian humorist Daniel Samper Pizano in his column "Postre de notas" (Carrusel 2003), says that proverbs urgently need to be revised because they are full of agricultural and craft references that only historians understand.

To this end he offers a series of modern day proverbs which, although written somewhat in jest could be future "old sayings". For example, *Si te hacen el atraco, no pelees con el caco* (When you are mugged, don't fight with the thug) or *Un potrero y balón, son la mejor religión* (An open field and a ball are the best religion of all). He has taken a reality of every day life, created a simple rhyme and makes it memorable by the truth it expresses. No doubt many of the "old sayings" we use today began in just this way.

Given the varied origins of proverbs, idioms and expressions, it is incumbent upon the interpreter to constantly acquire information relative to the culture of the languages in which he, or she works. From the perspective of learning a language, proverbs, idioms and expressions are essential to truly mastering any language. All reflect culture and people's attitude towards daily life. "Proverbs encapsulate popular wisdom" (Pérez, Sala and Santamaría, 290). Some are nearly identical in their translations. For instance, the equivalent in Spanish of the English proverb, *A bird in the hand is worth two in the bush,* is, *Más vale pájaro en mano que ciento volando. A* direct translation into English is, *A bird in the hand is better than a hundred flying.* In Arabic, the same proverb becomes, *A bird in your hand is better than ten in a tree.* The same idea in Somali is expressed as, *If you have fruit in your hand you don't have to pick the one in the tree.* My sources for these sayings, Mrs. Nazdar Hassan, (Arabic) and Mr. Sakawdin Mohamed, (Somali), report the constant use of proverbs in their respective languages and that children are taught in their native countries with the use of proverbs. Both commented that proverbs are known as "old people's sayings". This is consistent with my own experience as I often preface a proverb by saying "as my mother says…" and in English one hears frequently, " as the old saying goes…". This is an empirical indication that proverbs idioms and expressions are such an important part of language and cultural communication that we identify them as being part of our heritage even as we use them.

In conclusion, because proverbs idioms and expressions are used so frequently in the court setting, this reference guide will be very helpful to me, as well as to other interpreters. This guide also serves as a tribute to my mother.

English into Spanish

A

- **A bad padlock invites a picklock** – *La ocasión hace al ladrón.*
This saying warns us that if the situation is tempting enough, even the most honest person will be dishonest.

- **A bad penny always turns up** – *Hierba mala nunca muere.*
This saying makes allusion to the idea that something unwanted always reappears.

- **A barking dog seldom bites** – *Perro que ladra no muerde.*
We are advised by this short proverb that people who make a lot of noise about being tough are mostly all talk.

- **A bird in the hand is worth two in the bush** – *Más vale pájaro en mano que ciento volando.*
This saying advises us to take advantage of what we have even if it is less, or smaller, than what we might hope to get if we bypass what we have for sure.

- **A cat in mittens catches no mice** – *Gato con guantes no caza ratones.*
With this saying we are given to understand that some things are harder to accomplish if one has to be too careful.

- **A chain is only as strong as its weakest link** – *Siempre se quiebra la soga por lo más delgado.*
This expression refers to the dominance of the strong over the weak, the powerful over the helpless and the agile over the clumsy.

- **A chip off the old block** – *De tal palo tal astilla.*
The idea here is that a child has the same characteristics as the parent.

- **A dog bites the hand that feeds it** – *Cría cuervos y te sacarán los ojos.*
This is an expression of disappointment in someone who is ungrateful towards those who have been kind.

- **A fallen man is everybody's prey** – *Del árbol caído todos hacen leña.*
This saying makes a point of the ease with which people take advantage of someone who has fallen on hard times and is unable to defend himself.

- **A friend in need is a friend indeed** – *En el peligro se conoce el amigo.*
This saying means that a person who helps another, even in difficult times, is a true friend.

- **A jack of all trades, but master of none** – *Oficial de mucho, maestro de nada.*
This very common expression refers to people who claim to know how to do innumerable things, but in reality they do none of them well.

- **A leopard never changes its spots** – *Quien nace para burro, muere rebuznando.*
This expression refers to the fact that everybody is born with certain characteristics and that it is impossible to change them throughout life.

- **A little knowledge is a dangerous thing** – *La ignorancia es atrevida.*
No hay nada tan atrevido como la ignorancia.
This saying refers to those who know a little about something, but claim to know a great deal and are, therefore, dangerously ignorant.

- **A man is known by the company he keeps** – *Dime con quién andas y te diré quién eres.*
This saying refers to the fact that one can determine how another will act by watching the people with whom he keeps company.

- **A man's house is his castle** – *En mi casa estoy, rey soy.*
This expression tells us that, without question, someone in his own house makes the rules.

- **A new broom sweeps the best** – *Escoba nueva barre bien.*
This saying indicates that a new employee will seem to do everything right, while one who has been at the job for some time may not seem to do the same quality of work.

- **A rich man and his money are soon parted** – *La avaricia rompe el saco.*
This saying warns us that the desire to acquire more may, in fact, lead to the loss of what we have.

- **A rose by any other name is still a rose** – *Olivo y aceituno, todo es uno.*
This saying comes from Shakespeare's *What is in a Name?* and has moved into common speech to tell us that no matter what we call something, we can not change what it is.

- **A stitch in time saves nine** – *Remienda tu sayo y te durará un año, remiéndalo otra vez y te durará un mes.*
This expression indicates that prompt action avoids more serious trouble in the future.

- **A word to the wise is sufficient** – *Al buen entendedor con pocas palabras le bastan.*
This saying teaches us that an intelligent person will grasp the meaning without a long explanation.

- **Actions speak louder than words** – *Obras son amores y no buenas razones.*
This saying indicates that what you do is a lot more significant than what you say.

- **Add insult to injury** – *Tras de corneados, apaleados.*
Tras de cotudo, con paperas.
This saying is used to refer to people who suffer one bad event after another. It is said that a version of this saying appeared more than 2,000 years ago in the Fables of Phaedrus.

- **All that glitters is not gold** – *No todo lo que brilla es oro.*
  This saying advises one not to believe in appearances because appearances can be deceiving. Not everything that looks good always is good.

- **Always stand on your dignity** – *El que mucho se agachó hasta el culo se le vio.*
  This saying teaches that a person who confuses obedience with servitude loses his most precious possession, his dignity.

- **An eye for an eye and a tooth for a tooth** – *Ojo por ojo y diente por diente.*
  This proverb comes from the Bible. Deuteronomy 19:21 states, *"Life shall go for life, eye for eye, tooth for tooth."* It means that one is entitled to retaliate for an injury or an insult.

- **An ounce of prevention is worth a pound of cure** – *Más vale prevenir que tener que lamentar.*
  This saying tells us that it is better to keep something that is wrong from happening so it doesn't need to be fixed.

- **As the twig is bent, so grows the tree** – *Árbol que nace torcido, jamás su tronco endereza.*
  This proverb indicates that bad habits not corrected at an early age will continue throughout life.

- **As you judge, so shall you be judged** – *Con la vara con que midas, serás medido.*
  This proverb tells us that if we criticize others, we will, likewise, be criticized.

NOTES:_____

_____

_____

B

- **Bad things happen in the best of families** – *Al mejor cazador, se le va la liebre.*
  Al mejor panadero se le quema el pan.
  This saying expresses the idea that even the most expert and capable professionals can make a mistake.

- **Be good to everyone on your way up, because you never know whom you will meet on your way down** – *Arrieros somos y en el camino nos encontramos.*
  This saying tells us that we should be kind to everyone as we proceed through life because we may need to ask that person for a favor in the future.

- **Before you can say Jackie Robinson** – *En menos que canta un gallo.*
  This saying refers to the speed with which something can happen or how quickly a job can be done.

- **Before you marry be sure of a house wherein to tarry** – *El que se casa quiere casa y costal para la plaza.*
  This saying advises that a married couple should have their own house and not share living quarters with others.

- **Beggars can't be choosers** – *Con buen hambre no hay mal pan.*
  We are reminded by this saying that if one is sufficiently in need, anything will do.

- **Better late than never** – *Más vale tarde que nunca.*
  This proverb is used as an excuse for being late, or as a gesture of civility by the person who has been kept waiting. This proverb is found in Chaucer's *Canterbury Tales* (1410) as *"Bet than never is late."*

- **Better safe than sorry** – *Más vale prevenir que curar.*
  This proverb advises one to be careful, to stay away from obvious risks, and to avoid disasters.

- **Better the devil you know than the devil you don't** – *Más vale malo conocido que bueno por conocer.*
  Vale más malo conocido que bueno por conocer.
  This proverb tell us that we should be happy with what we know, even if it does not appear to be as good as something else.

- **Better to ask the way than to go astray** – *Preguntando se va a Roma.*
  This saying teaches us that we can avoid being ignorant by simply asking questions to find out the correct answers.

- **Better to be a big fish in a small pond, than a small fry in the ocean** – *Más vale ser cabeza de ratón que cola de león.*
  This saying demonstrates the possible advantages one may have by being influential in a small area, rather than by being just one of many in a bigger place.

- **Better to be alone than in bad company** – *Más vale solo que mal acompañado.*
  This expression says it is preferable to be by oneself, instead of being surrounded by people we do not like.

- **Better to be embarrassed once, than to have regrets forever** – *Más vale una vez colorado que ciento descolorido.*
  This expression reminds us that it is always best to confront a difficult situation squarely and up front, rather than to regret not having acted.

- **Bigger is always better** – *Caballo grande, ande o no ande.*
  This saying demonstrates that some people always want the biggest of everything, without any regard to its quality.

- **Birds of a feather flock together** – *Cada oveja con su pareja.*
  Dios los cría y ellos se juntan.
  Los caballos viejos se buscan para rascarse.
  Nunca falta un roto para un descosido.
  This saying refers to the fact that people with similar views or interests associate with one another. It is based on the observation that a group of birds on the ground or flying are often all of the same species.

- **Breeding will out** – *Como no ha aprendido a ser señora se resbala del cojín.*
  En la mesa y en el juego se conoce al caballero.
  This expression says that one is able to judge a person's social level by his or her manners and education.

- **Business before pleasure** – *Primero está la obligación que la devoción.*
  This saying reiterates that our commitment to work should come before our inclination to seek fun.

NOTES:_____

_____

_____

C

- **Call a spade a spade** – *Al pan, pan y al vino, vino.*
  This saying is a mistranslation of an ancient Greek saying, I call a fig a fig, a spade a spade, but nevertheless it directs one to speak plainly and directly.

- **Cloak-and-dagger** – *De capa y espada*
  This expression dates back to a 16th century Spanish phrase describing plays by Lope de Vega and Calderon de la Barca, which were full of spying, fights and adventures and in which the actor wore a cloak that usually concealed a sword or dagger. Today the expression is used to refer to the dramatic intrigue of secret operations.

- **Come hell or high water** – *Contra viento y marea.*
  This saying speaks to the need to achieve a goal at all costs, no matter the consequences that may occur or the obstacles that may be encountered.

- **Comfort is better than pride** – *Ande yo caliente, y ríase la gente.*
  This saying reminds us that one must take care of one's own needs and not consider what others may think or say.

NOTES:_____

_____

_____

D

- **Do as I say, not as I do** – *El cura predica, pero no aplica.*
  It recommends that we follow instructions and not imitate behavior.

- **Do good and dread no shame** – *Haz el bien y no mires a quien.*
  This expression reminds us to do good deeds impartially and
  without a view towards reward.

- **Do unto others as you would have them do unto you** – *No
  hagas mal que esperes bien.*
  This well-known Golden Rule has versions that are cited several
  times in the Bible, most notably in Matthew 7:12, where Jesus
  taught that everyone must treat each other with respect and love.

- **Don't bite off more than you can chew** – *El que mucho abarca,
  poco aprieta.*
  This saying advises us not to take on a task that is a lot more than
  what we can do or handle. It came about from seeing children
  ingest large amount of food at once, without being able to chew
  it. It was first recorded in the United States at the end of the 19th
  century.

- **Don't cast pearls before swine** – *La miel no se hizo para la jeta
  del asno.*
  This partial quote from the Sermon on the Mount (as recorded in
  Matthew 7:6 *"Do not give dogs what is holy; and do not throw pearls
  before swine,…"*) refers to offering something valuable to a person
  who is incapable of appreciating it.

- **Don't criticize your brother until you have walked a mile in his
  shoes** – *Nadie sabe el pan que se amasa en casa, ni la vida que
  se pasa.*
  This saying reiterates that appearances are deceiving. One cannot
  know the difficulties that others have suffered without having had
  the same experiences.

- **Don't pee on my leg and tell me it is raining** – *A otro perro con ese hueso.*
  This rather pithy statement recommends that one not attempt to lie to someone who is more knowledgeable.

  _____

- **Don't put the cart before the horse** – *No hay que ensillar antes de traer las bestias.*
  This ancient proverb first appeared in English in 1340 and teaches that things should be done in the correct order. Figuratively speaking, it reminds us not to get ahead of ourselves.

  _____

- **Don't wash your dirty linen in public** – *La ropa sucia se lava en casa.*
  This teaching reminds us that family problems should be resolved within the family and not in public. It can also be applied to problems that may arise at the work place.

  _____

- **Dressed to the nines** – *Estar de veinticinco alfileres.*
  The expression indicates that one is impressively attired. A possible theory for this expression that dates from the 1700 relates to nine being the highest single digit and thus it is defined as the best.

  _____

  NOTES:_____

  _____

  _____

E

- **Easy come, easy go** – *Lo que por agua viene, por agua se va.*
This ancient proverb and several other versions of it simply state that things for which we have made no effort to obtain can also disappear without effort.

- **Enough is enough** – *Bueno es culantro pero no tanto.*
This short saying implies that there is a limit to everything, whether it is good or bad.

- **Every cloud has a silver lining** – *No hay mal que por bien no venga.*
The cloud in this proverb is the metaphor used for life's difficult situations and the silver lining is the positive result that can come from every negative happening.

- **Every dog has its day** – *A cada puerco le llega su San Martín.*
This proverb can be interpreted in one of two ways. The first refers to the fact that even the "lowest" person can have a moment of happiness. The other implies that justice will finally arrive as a punishment for a bad deed.

- **Every Jack must have his Jill** – *Cada oveja con su pareja.*
Tal para cual, María para Juan.
This saying states that somewhere there is a match for everyone, and that each person should therefore look for someone who is his or her equal.

- **Every little bit helps** – *Un grano no hace granero, pero ayuda al compañero.*
This expression teaches that any contribution, no matter how small, can help a lot.

- **Everyone gets their just deserts** – *A cada puerco le llega su San Martín.*
This expression reminds us that, sooner or later, we all get exactly what we deserve, whether it is good or bad. The obsolete word *deserts*, which dates to the 1300's, is only used in this expression today.

- **Everyone has a little larceny in his heart** – *En arca abierta, el justo peca.*
This saying reminds us that many times people do bad things just because opportunity presents itself.

NOTES:_____

_____

_____

F

- **Failure teaches success** – *Echando a pique se aprende.*
  This expression teaches us that the only thing we learn from success is success itself, but that failure shows us what to avoid in order to be successful.

- **Finders keepers, losers weepers** – *El que se fue a Sevilla perdió su silla.*
  This saying indicates that if you leave your post or if you lose something, whoever takes over or finds what is lost has the right to call it his own.

- **Fine feathers make fine birds** – *Por el equipaje se conoce al pasajero.*
  This saying reminds us that people are judged by appearances with no regard for the character and values they possess.

- **Fools rush in where angels fear to tread** – *El necio es atrevido y el sabio comedido.*
  This saying reiterates that sometimes ignorant or inexperienced people get into a situation that a more experienced or wiser person would avoid completely.

- **Forewarned is forearmed** – *Hombre prevenido vale por dos.*
  This expression demonstrates that being aware of something in advance allows one to be prepared.

- **Fortune is wasted on fools** – *A los bobos se les aparece la Virgen.*
  This brief adage observes that often times those least capable of appreciating good luck have it dropped in their lap.

- **Fortune smiles on some, but not on others** – *Unos nacen con estrella y otros nacen estrellados.*
  Some people are born under a lucky star and no matter what they do, it always ends well for them, while others seem incapable of doing well, no matter how much they try.

NOTES:_____

_____

_____

G

Get on a high horse – *Subírsele los humos a la cabeza.*
This expression refers to a person who acts in a superior or arrogant way. It alludes to the use of tall horses for important officials to ride during processions, thus emphasizing their rank in society.

Give a dog a bad name – *Cría fama y échate a dormir.*
This saying warns us that we are judged by our behavior, and even if we change, that previous behavior will always follow us.

Give him an inch, and he will take a mile – *Le da el pie y se toma la mano.*
This expression reminds us that there are people who will take advantage of you if you show them some kindness and do favors for them.

God helps those who help themselves – *Ayúdate que yo te ayudaré.*
This old proverb teaches us that we should make an effort on our own behalf instead of waiting for God or someone else to do everything for us.

God tempers the wind to the unshorn lamb – *Dios aprieta pero no ahoga.*
This saying means that even though we sometimes suffer, God is merciful and is not going to abandon us.

Grin and bear it – *Al mal tiempo, buena cara.*
This expression states that when we encounter a bad or difficult situation, we should make the best of that situation with good humor, since there is little or nothing that can be done about it. This saying became very popular in the 19th century to the point that Sam Walter Foss incorporated it in the title of his poem "The Firm of Grin and Barrett".

NOTES:_____

_____

_____

H

- **Half a loaf is better than none** – *A falta de pan buenas son tortas.*
  This old proverb says that it is better to get part of that for which you are aiming, than to not get anything at all. The proverbs dates from 1546, when it was *"For better is half a loaf than no bread."*

- **Hard living leads to a bad end** – *Quien mal anda, mal acaba.*
  The warning inherent in this old saying is that debauchery will put us in the grave at an early age. It was personified in the late 1960's by the life of rock star Jim Morrison who exhorted a generation to *"Live hard, die young,"* which he did.

- **Haste makes waste** – *De la carrera no queda sino el cansancio.*
  Piano, piano se va lontano.
  This proverb warns that to do things in a hurry and impulsively can spoil the results. In John Ray's 1678 collection of proverbs, he recorded the entire warning: "Haste makes waste, and waste makes want, and want makes strife between the goodman and his wife."

- **He doesn't know if he is afoot or on horseback** – *Está entre ecuestre y pedestre.*
  This expression refers to a person who, because of confusion or indecision, does not know what to think or do.

- **He was caught red-handed** – *Lo agarraron con las manos en la masa.*
  The reference in this expression is to people who are apprehended in the act of doing something that they shouldn't do.

- **He who goes to the fair, loses his chair** – *El que va a Quito, pierde su banquito.*
  El que se fue a Sevilla, perdió su silla.
  This expression says that a person who is absent from a position (i.e. a job) can expect that others will supplant him while he is gone.

- **He who laughs last laughs best** – *El que ríe de ultimo, ríe mejor.*
  This saying refers to those who achieve success after several
  failures and the danger of making fun of others because, in the end,
  they may come out on top.

- **He who lives by the sword so shall he die by the sword** – *Quien
  a hierro mata a hierro muere.*
  This ancient proverb means that the harsh treatment of others will
  be repaid in kind. It originally comes from the Bible. St Matthew
  26:52 says: *"All who take the sword will perish by the sword."*

- **His bark is worse than his bite** – *Perro ladrador, poco mordedor.*
  This saying implies that a loud, aggressive person is all noise and
  very little *danger.*

- **Hot air** – *Palabras al aire.*
    Palabras al viento.
  This expression refers to promises easily and often given, but
  seldom met. It is also a metaphor for exaggerations that dissipate
  like steam.

NOTES:_____

_____

_____

I

- **If the shoe fits, wear it** – *Al que le caiga el guante que se lo plante.*
  This saying tells us if something negative is said and applies to you, accept it. Originally the saying was "if the cap fits, put it on," referring to the fool's cap. The new version, however, is more common perhaps because of the Cinderella fairy tale, in which the prince searches for Cinderella by trying her lost glass slipper on the feet of all the young maidens in his domain.

- **If you can't take the heat, stay out of the kitchen** – *El que tenga rabo de paja que no se arrime a la candela.*
  This saying, which means if one cannot stand the stress of a situation, one must leave or give up, is attributed to President Harry Truman and dates from the 1950's.

- **If you lie down with dogs, you are going to get up with fleas** –
  Quien con lobos anda, a aullar aprende.
      El que con niños se acuesta, orinado amanece.
  This expression says that those who mix with undesirable company will pick up undesirable traits.

- **If you stoop too low, your ass will show** – *El que mucho se agachó hasta el culo se le vio.*
  This saying refers to some people who confuse obedience with servility and loose their dignity in the process.

- **Ignorance is bliss** – *Ojos que no ven, corazón que no siente.*
  This expression says that if you are not aware of something it cannot hurt you. The actual quote for this saying comes from "Odd on a Distant Prospect of Eton College" by Thomas Gray, 1742. "Where ignorance is bliss, 'tis folly to be wise."

- **In every country dogs bite** – *Dondequiera se cuecen habas.*
      Dondequiera hay faldriquera teniendo las naguas rotas.
  This expression says that wherever we go we will see the same things happening throughout the world.

In the blink of an eye – *En un abrir y cerrar de ojos.*
This saying is a reminder of how quickly things can happen.

In the land of the blind, the one-eyed man is king – *En tierra de ciegos, el tuerto es rey.*
This expression says that in a group of ignorant people, anyone who has only slightly more knowledge or intelligence than the rest can easily become the leader of the group.

In two shakes of a lamb's tail – *En menos que canta un gallo.*
This allusion to the agility and quick movements of lambs is a metaphor for how quickly things can happen.

It is a red herring – *Es un despiste.*
This idiom alludes to the practice of dragging a strong smelling smoked herring across the trail in order to cover the scent to throw off tracking dogs.

It is better to reign in Hell than to serve in Heaven – *Más vale ser cabeza de ratón que cola de león.*
This proverb tells us that it is more satisfying to be the first among a few than one among many.

It is easier said than done – *Del dicho al hecho hay mucho trecho.*
This saying teaches that it is easier to promise to do something than to actually carry out the promise.

It is no use crying over spilt milk – *A lo hecho, pecho.*
This saying, with its reference to a common domestic accident, tells us not to dwell on what might have been, but to accept it and move forward.

It is the master's eye that makes the mill go – *Al ojo del amo engorda el caballo.*
This saying reminds us that the best results are obtained if the owner looks after his own possessions and business personally.

- **It never rains, but it pours** – *Si por allá llueve por aquí no escampa.*
  This old expression reminds us that when problems appear, they come in overwhelming amounts. It may come from a 1726 book by Jonathan Swift entitled "It cannot rain but it pours."

- **It takes all sorts to make a world** – *De todo hay en la viña del Señor.*
  This saying teaches us that the world is made up of many types of people and elements, and they all contribute to the colorful mosaic of human life.

- **It's always useful to have a friend in high places** – *Quien a buen árbol se arrima, buena sombra le cobija.*
  This expression refers to the advantages that occur for those who enjoy the protection of someone in a position of power.

- **It's an ill wind that blows nobody any good** – *En río revuleto, ganancia de pescadores.*
  This proverb refers to any loss being of benefit to someone. The full version can be found in a 1546 collection of proverbs by John Heywood.

- **It's better to be embarrassed once than to have regrets forevermore** – *Más vale una vez colorado que ciento descolorido.*
  This expression says that it is preferable to face a difficult situation firmly and not worry about the embarrassment that may occur.

- **It's not a crime to steal from a thief** – *Ladrón que roba un ladrón tiene cien años de perdón.*
  This expression is used as an excuse to justify a bad deed committed against those who commit bad deeds.

- **It's the last straw that breaks the camel's back** – *Éramos pocos y parió la abuela.*
      Se llenó la copa.
  This saying states that there is a limit to everything and beyond that limit, things go wrong.

NOTES:_____

_____

_____

J

- **Jack of all trades** – *Aprendiz de mucho, maestro de nada.*
  This proverb teaches that a person should concentrate on only one job at a time, since trying to learn too many things one ends up not doing any of them well.

- **Judge not a book by its cover** – *No juzguéis la pieza por la muestra.*
  This saying reminds us not to consider only the superficial when deciding a value of a person or thing.

- **Judge not that ye be not judged** – *No juzguéis para que no seáis juzgados.*
  Also from the proliferation of sayings coming from Jesus' Sermon on the Mount, this proverb admonishes us not to judge or criticize others, for they likewise will criticize us.

NOTES:_____

_____

_____

K

- **Keep a stiff upper lip** – *Al mal tiempo, buena cara.*
  This expression says that we must accept bad times and do our best, since we can't change them.

- **Keep your nose out of other people's business** – *Agua que no has de beber, déjala correr.*
  This saying reminds us not to pry or meddle in things that do not concern us.

NOTES:_____

_____

_____

L

- **Laws are made to be broken** – *Hecha la ley, hecha la trampa.*
  This expression says that every law passed is a challenge to
  someone to break it. These few words describe the real truth about
  man's attempt to organize his society with laws and rules.

- **Least said, soonest mended** – *El que mucho habla. mucho yerra.*
  Por la boca muere el pez.
  This proverb praises the ability to hold one's tongue and keep quiet
  instead of telling all.

- **Lemmings go blindly down to the sea** – *Ovejas bobas, por do va
  una, van todas.*
  This expression describes people who follow the example of
  others without thinking. The reference here is to the supposed
  phenomenon of a Northern European rodent that throws itself into
  the sea for apparently no better reason than to follow others who
  have done so.

- **Let he who has no sins cast the first stone** – *El que esté libre de
  culpa que tire la primera piedra.*
  This expression from the Bible (St. John 8:7) reminds us that we are
  all sinners and as such, we should not criticize others for being what
  we ourselves are.

- **Life is not just a bowl of cherries** – *No todo el monte es orégano.*
  This saying signifies that life isn't all that easy. It is a new saying
  in English, dating from the 1930's. It is the widespread negative
  version of a song title by Brown and Henderson "Life is just a bowl
  of cherries."

- **Like coal to Newcastle** – *Cargar leña al monte.*
  This metaphor is used to describe an action that is superfluous and
  therefore useless. Newcastle was a famous English coal-mining
  area for several centuries, so bringing coal to Newcastle was a
  useless gesture.

- **Like leading lambs to the slaughter** – *Como corderos al matadero.*
  This expression makes reference to people who follow the example of others without realizing the danger ahead.

- **Like lemmings to the sea** – *Ovejas bobas, por do va una, van todas.*
  This expression describes people who follow the example of others without thinking. The reference here is to the supposed phenomenon of a Northern European rodent that throws itself into the sea for apparently no better reason than to follow others who have done so.

- **Look before you leap** – *Antes de que te cases, mira lo que haces.*
  This proverb teaches us to think about the consequences of our actions before we act. It is found in Aesop's Fables, referring to the fox that can't get out of a well but convinces a goat to jump in. The fox crawls out over the back of the goat and the goat becomes the one trapped in the well.

- **Look not for the speck in your brother's eye, but for the log in your own eye** – *Vemos la paja en el ojo ajeno, pero no la viga que tenemos en el propio.*
  This saying has its origin in the New Testament Book of Matthew (7:3,5), which asks the question: "Why do you see the speck in your brother's eye, but do not notice the log that is in your own eye?" This refers to the ease with which people ignore their own defects but notice the smallest defects in others.

- **Looking for a needle in a haystack** – *Buscar una aguja en un pajal.*
  This saying indicates how difficult, if not impossible, it is sometimes to locate one item or one individual among many.

NOTES:_____

_____

_____

M

- **Make hay while the sun shines** – *A la ocasión la pintan calva.*
  This saying tells us to take advantage of every favorable moment.
  By itself, it alludes to the difficulty that farmers face in putting up the
  hay while the weather is dry so it doesn't spoil.

- **Man does not live by bread alone** – N*o sólo de pan vive el
  hombre.*
  The common understanding of this expression is that physical
  subsistence is not enough to sustain the human spirit. The original
  Biblical quote is from St. Matthew 4:4: *Man shall not live by bread
  alone, but by every word that proceedeth out the mouth of God.*

- **Man proposes and God disposes** – *El hombre propone y Dios
  dispone.*
  This saying reminds us that reaching our goals depends on God's
  will. No matter what we plan to do, if God does not agree, it won't
  happen.

- **Many a mickel makes a muckle** – *De grano en grano llena la
  gallina el buche.*
  This seemingly nonsensical proverb uses alliteration and Scottish
  variations of the word *much* to tell us that small continued
  savings will eventually lead to riches or that great deeds can be
  accomplished in small steps.

- **Many are called, few are chosen** – *Muchos son los llamados y
  pocos los escogidos.*
  This well-known proverb says that many people may aspire to a
  goal, but only a small number will achieve it. This proverb comes
  from Mathew 22:14.

- **Marriages are made in heaven** – *Matrimonio y mortaja, del cielo
  bajan.*
  This proverb says that whom we marry is out of our control and
  subject to the will of God. In a more figurative and mundane sense,
  it means we are not the masters of our own destiny.

- **Might makes right** – *¿Al alcalde quien lo ronda?*
  This saying, dating from the 14th century, states that those who have the power make the rules by which others must live.

- **Mind your own business** – *Coma, calle y no pregunte de dónde sale.*
  Zapatero a tus zapatos
  This simple admonition reminds us not to meddle in the affairs of others.

- **Misery loves company** – *El que se queja, sus males aleja.*
  This expression says that having others suffer with us somehow eases the pain. Its earliest use in English dates to the mid-14th century.

- **Money talks** – *Poderoso caballero es don dinero.*
  This expression describes the great influence of wealth. Although the current version of this truism came in the 1900's, the basis for this idiom is found as far back as the 5th century B.C.

NOTES:_____

_____

_____

N

- **Never bite the hand that feeds you** – *Al que se le come el pan se le reza el padrenuestro.*
  This metaphor of a dog biting its master refers to people who are ungrateful towards those that have shown them kindness or given them some benefit.

- **Never look a gift horse in the mouth** – *A caballo regalado no se le mira el colmillo.*
  This saying reminds us not to be ungrateful for gifts or suspicious of the giver. The allusion is to the horse trader's custom of checking a horse's teeth to determine its age. The saying dates as far back as the 4th century.

- **Never put off until tomorrow what can be done today** – *No dejes para mañana lo que puedas hacer hoy.*
  This proverb, first recorded in Chaucer's *Tale of the Melibee*, recommends that we not delay in doing those things which can be done immediately.

- **Never say never** – *Nunca diga de esta agua no beberé, porque le toca ahogarse en ella.*
  This short saying implies that we should never deny the possibility that there are things we might have to do in the future, even though we may not like it.

- **Never spit into the wind** – *El que escupe a lo alto, a la cara le cae.*
  This expression refers to evil deeds coming back to haunt us.

- **No dish pleases all palates alike** – *Cada uno cuenta de la feria según le va en ella.*
  This expression reminds us that everyone sees things from his or her own point of view. No two eyewitnesses tell the same story.

- **No one knows the troubles that others have seen** – *Nadie sabe la sed con que otro bebe.*
  This saying reiterates that no one can truly judge the needs of others.

- **No pain, no gain** – *El que quiere marrones que aguante tirones.*
  This short saying, quite popular in athletic circles, refers to the need to struggle through unpleasantness in order to reach a goal.

- **Not to know the difference between his ass and a hole in the ground** – *Confundir el culo con las témporas.*
  This expression is used to comment on those who are detached from reality or so challenged that they do not understand simple concepts.

- **Nothing ventured, nothing gained** – *El que quiere celeste que le cueste.*
  No se pescan truchas a bragas enjutas.
  El que quiere marrones que aguante tirones.
  This adage, first recorded in the 1600's, tells us that it is necessary to take some risks in order to achieve a goal.

NOTES:_____

_____

_____

O

- **Old habits die hard** – *Difícil cosa es dejar lo acostumbrado.*
  This expression emphasizes how difficult it is to change any ingrained behavior or habit.

- **Once bitten, twice shy** – *Gato escaldado del agua fría huye.*
  This saying reminds us that a bad experience makes one more cautious the second time around.

- **One can't make an omelet without breaking some eggs** – *El que no arriesga un huevo, no tiene un pollo.*
  This saying teaches us that it is not possible to achieve a desired goal without taking some risks.

- **One good turn deserves another** – *Amor con amor se paga.*
  In this adage, the word turn is synonymous with a favor. A favor done for someone, therefore, deserves another in return.

- **One law for oneself, another for everyone else** – *La ley del embudo: lo ancho para ellos y lo angosto para uno.*
  This expression indicates how we apply not only the law, but also our point of view, to any given situation, taking into account our own interests first.

- **One man's meat is another man's poison** – *Entre gustos no hay disgustos.*
  This saying says that not everyone enjoys the same things. Tastes are different, and what is enjoyed by one person is not necessarily enjoyed by another.

- **One nail drives out another** – *Un clavo saca otro clavo o ambos se quedan adentro.*
  This expression says that the best way to overcome an adversity is when another one appears and replaces it. Another potential meaning is that of revenge against someone who has done us wrong.

- **Only the good die young** – *Hierba mala nunca muere.*
  This expression makes reference to the innocence of youth always being destroyed by death or by gaining enough experience and cynicism in order to survive into old age.

- **Out of sight, out of mind** – *Ojos que no ven, corazón que no siente.*
  This proverb says that if people don't see you, they are going to overlook you. It also implies that we soon forget the things we don't see.

- **Out of the frying pan, into the fire** –.*Salir de Guatemala y meterse en guatepeor.*
  Huyendo del trueno cayó en el relámpago.
  This expression implies that a person has gotten out of a bad situation only to get into another that is much worse. An earlier expression recorded in English in 1528 stated: "Lepe the like a flounder out of a frying-pane into the fyre."

NOTES:_____

_____

_____

P

- **Politeness is not a sign of weakness** – *Lo cortés no quita lo valiente.*
  This expression teaches us that good manners and kindness are never a problem. Quite the opposite, they are the first line of defense for our convictions and our ideals.

- **Poverty breeds discontent** – *Donde no hay harina, todo es mohina.*
  This proverb tells us that poverty causes people to be unhappy and constantly irritated because of their economic situation.

- **Practice makes perfect** – *Echando a pique se aprende.*
  This expression says that in order to become proficient at any endeavor, repetition is necessary.

- **Practice what you preach** – *El cura predica pero no aplica.*
  This brief admonition makes the point that one should follow the advice that one gives to another. To do otherwise is hypocrisy.

- **Put your faith in God and keep your powder dry** – *A Dios rogando y con el mazo dando.*
  This saying reminds us that no matter how strong your belief that a higher power will take care of you, it is imperative to be ready to take care of yourself.

NOTES:_____

_____

_____

R

- **Red sun in the morning, sailors take warning** – *Arreboles al oriente, aguas al día siguiente.*
  This weather-related adage simply states that bad sailing weather is in the offing.

- **Render unto Caesar that which is Caesar's and unto God that which is God's** – *Al César lo que es del César y a Dios lo que es de Dios.*
  This quote from Jesus in Matthew 22:23 has come to mean that we should give to others what is justly due them.

- **Rome wasn't built in a day** – *No se ganó Zamora en una hora.*
  We are advised by this saying to be patient in all our endeavors. It makes us remember that Rome, the greatest city of its day, lasted for centuries, but it also took centuries to build.

NOTES:_____

_____

_____

S

- **Seeing is believing** – *Ver y creer, dijo Santo Tomás.*
  This expression reminds us that we should always see proof of what we hear in order to confirm its veracity.

- **Servants make the worst masters** – *No hay cuña que más apriete que la del mismo palo.*
  This saying teaches us that sometimes the people who are closest to us are the most dangerous, and it is they who can do us the most harm.

- **Silence gives consent** – *El que calla otorga.*
  This short saying comments on the propensity of people to let things happen without protest. It also brings to mind the idea of an acquiescent electorate inherent in the phrase, *"The Silent Majority,"* which was popular during the Presidency of Richard Nixon.

- **Silence is golden** – *En boca cerrada no entra mosca.*
  We are advised by this saying to be discreet and to know when to keep quiet.

- **Six of one, and half a dozen of the other** – *Una de cal y otra de arena.*
  This saying is commonly used to express the idea that one thing is just as good as another. In today's world, one often hears the same idea stated in one word, "Whatever…"

- **Slow and steady wins the race** – *El que menos corre, vuela.*
  Harking back to Aesop's fable of *The Turtle and the Hare,* this proverb tells us that keeping a steady pace, however slow, will get us to the finish line ahead of those who jump off to a quick start and then run out of energy.

- **Soon ripe, soon rotten** – *Sol que mucho madruga, poco dura.*
  In the figurative sense, this expression says that things done quickly, and without preparation, often end in failure.

- **Sow the wind and reap the whirlwind** – *El que siembra vientos recoge tempestades.*
  As with many enduring proverbs, this saying comes from the Scriptures, specifically Hosea 8:7 and teaches that we are destined to suffer the consequences of our bad actions.

- **Spare the rod and spoil the child** – *Madre pía, daño cría. La letra con sangre entra.*
  Often used in reference to harsh teaching methods, this proverb supposes that physical discipline is better than permissive indulgence in raising children.

- **Speak of the angels and you hear their wings flapping** – *Hablando del Rey de Roma y él que asoma.*
  This saying is used in describing what seems to be the predetermined appearance of a person at the moment when their name is mentioned in conversation. Although it is most likely a coincidental occurrence, the reference to "angels" enhances the feeling that it is a providential phenomenon.

- **Stand up and take your medicine** – *A lo hecho, pecho*
  This idiomatic phrase advises us that we must assume responsibility for our actions and face the consequences with courage.

- **Sticks and stones may break my bones, but names will never hurt me** – *Maldición de gallinazo nunca llega al espinazo.*
  Frequently used as a lesson for children, this proverb teaches that insults are usually as empty as the people who use them and they cannot really do us any harm.

- **Still waters run deep** – *Del agua mansa líbrame Dios que de la brava me libraré yo.*
  This saying tells us that it is impossible to know what is actually occurring when everything seems calm. Likewise, many times people who show no emotion are the most dangerous, so we should, perhaps, be cautious of them.

- **Strike while the iron is hot** – *Dígale cotudo antes de que él se lo diga.*
  This proverb advises us to take advantage of the moment so as not to lose out on an opportunity.

  _____

  NOTES:_____

  _____

  _____

T

- **Tell it to the Marines** – *A otro perro con ese hueso.*
  This is an expression of disbelief or incredulity, and comes from a time when sailors thought that Marines were of no use. Lord Byron used a line with a similar idea in a footnote to *The Island: "That will do for the marines, but the sailors won't believe it."*

- **That's another kettle of fish** – *Ese es otro cantar.*
  This rather "folksy" saying refers to the character of something being totally different from another even if there is some similarity.

- **The apple never falls far from the tree** – *Hijo de tigre sale pintado.*
  This adage uses the physical truth about where ripe apples hit the ground when they fall off the tree. Figuratively it applies to the idea that one can expect children to be very much like their parents.

- **The best cure is the hair of the dog that bit you** – *No hay mejor cirujano que el acuchillado.*
  While this maxim is sometimes used to mean that there is no replacement for experience, its more common use is to imply that drinking an alcoholic beverage is the best cure for a hangover.

- **The big fish swallows up the little one** – *El pez grande se come al chico.*
  This saying relies on a truth that exists in nature and warns the small and weak to run when they try to deal with the large and powerful.

- **The blind leading the blind** – *Ovejas bobas, por do va una, van todas.*
  This expression describes people who follow the example of others without thinking.

- **The clothes don't make the man** – *El hábito no hace al monje.*
  This saying tells us not to judge people by what we can see of them on the outside because we can be fooled by appearances.

- **The coast is clear** – *No hay moros en la costa.*
  Literally this saying, at one time, meant that there was no danger along the coastline, so it was safe to come ashore. Over time this saying has been adapted to mean, that no one is watching or listening.

- **The Devil looks after his own** – *Yerba mala nunca muere.*
  Bicho malo nunca muere.
  This adage states that the worst people seem to have a guardian angel (the Devil) that does not allow bad things happen to them. It is somewhat of a paraphrase of the famous quote by baseball's late Leo Durocher, *"Nice guys finish last."*

- **The early bird catches the worm** – *El que más madrugó una bolsa de oro se encontró.*
  A quien madruga Dios le ayuda.
  This very common saying teaches us that getting up early to accomplish one's work is the best way to achieve success. Nobody talks about the fact that getting up early did nothing at all for the worm.

- **The first step in any journey is always the most difficult** – *El comer y el rascar el trabajo es comenzar.*
  The truth in this saying is that getting started is the biggest obstacle to accomplishing any task and ninety-nine percent of any job is just doing the work.

- **The gods send nuts to those who have no teeth** – *Dios le da pan a quien no tiene dientes.*
  This proverb alludes to the belief that some people have things that they are incapable of enjoying.

- **The hand that gave the wound, must give the cure** – *Dios da la llaga, pero da la medicina.*
This proverb tells us that cure for common sufferings is found with those who cause them.

- **The leopard can't change his spots** – *Genio y figura hasta la sepultura.*
This maxim refers to a person who is of an inalterable character and who will never change during his entire life.

- **The lesser of two evils** – *De los males, el menos.*
This idiomatic phrase refers to needing to accept a choice between two negative, but unavoidable, alternatives.

- **The longest day must have an end** – *No hay mal que dure cien años ni cuerpo que lo resista.*
This expression states that no matter how difficult anything is, everything eventually passes because nothing lasts forever.

- **The more you have, the more you want** – *Quien más tiene, más quiere.*
This truism, which seems especially applicable in these days of Enron, WolrldCom and mutual fund scandal makes reference to the very universal human weakness of greed.

- **The only sure things are death and taxes** – *Para todo hay remedio, menos para la muerte.*
This old saying is sometimes used to express hope when there seems to be no solution to a problem.

- **The road to hell is paved with good intentions** – *De buenas intenciones está empedrado el infierno.*
This Scottish proverb teaches us that no matter how much we want to do something, the desire is totally useless if we don't follow through with definite action.

- **The same music with a different tune** – *El mismo perro con distinto collar.*
  This metaphorical expression is often applied to political promises and usually means that even though things appear to change, the same behavior continues on.

- **The shoemaker's children go barefoot** – *En casa de carpintero, puerta de cuero.*
  En casa de herrero, azadón de palo.
  This saying tells us that we do not always find things where we would most expect to find them. It can also mean that a person with a particular ability, or skill, often does not use his ability, or skill, for his own well-being.

- **The shortest way to a man's heart is through his stomach** – *Barriga llena, corazón contento.*
  This saying speaks to the satisfaction that one feels after having eaten well. It also means that the best way to obtain a favor from someone is by feeding that person. In some circles it is known as "the power of the tortilla."

- **The squeaky wheel gets the grease** – *El que no llora no mama.*
  This saying expresses the truth in human nature that if you want to draw attention to a problem, or to an objective, you have to make noise.

- **The truth will out** – *Peleando las comadres se descubren las verdades.*
  This short saying warns us that no matter how hard we try to hide something, the truth will always become known.

- **There are none so deaf as those who will not hear** – *No hay peor sordo que el que no quiere oír.*
  This proverb expresses the idea that no matter how hard one may try, it is impossible to change the mind of a stubborn person who will not listen to reason.

- **There is honor among thieves** – *Entre bueyes no hay cornadas. Perro no come perro.*
  This saying expresses the widely held belief that people with the same disrespectful character hold each other in mutual respect either because they are peers, or out of fear.

- **There is many a slip betwixt cup and lip** – *Del dicho al hecho hay mucho trecho.*
  Del plato a la boca se enfría la sopa.
  De la mano a la boca, se pierde la sopa.
  This proverb warns that promises are easy to make but difficult to carry out. It can also mean that all hope of reaching a goal can be wiped out in a second.

- **There is no consolation in being in the same boat with other fools** – *Mal de muchos, consuelo de tontos.*
  The reference in this expression is that commiserating with others who find themselves in the same unfortunate situation does no one any good.

- **There is no great loss without some gain** – *Perder por conocer no es perder.*
  This saying is meant to show that even if we fail at some endeavor, we will always learn something from the failure.

- **There is no rest for the wicked** – *A dónde va el buey que no are.*
  This saying is often used as a comment on the need to work long hours just to stay ahead. Isaiah 57:21 says, "There is no peace, says my God for the wicked." The essence of this saying, however, comes from Genesis 3:17. After God has driven Adam and Eve from the Garden He says, "Cursed is the ground because of you; in toil you shall eat of it all the days of your life."

- **There is no rose without a thorn** – *No hay miel sin hiel.*
  We are reminded by this short saying that anything worthwhile is only achieved with pain.

- **There is no substitute for experience** – *Sabe más el diablo por viejo que por diablo.*
  This common expression implies that although education and training are good and necessary, they are not much good without experience.

- **There is nothing like freedom** – *El buey suelto bien se lame.*
  This statement praises the idea that being your own person, and being able to live as you please, is a powerful human desire.

- **There is nothing like the old horse for the hard road** – *Más sabe el diablo por viejo que por diablo.*
  This proverb uses metaphors to state that, "There is no substitute for experience."

- **There is nothing that money can't buy** – *Por la plata baila el perro.*
  This expression means that although cynical in its frankness, this old saying is probably truer than we would like to admit. The desire for money drives most of our actions.

- **There is one law for the rich and another for the poor** – *La ley es para los de ruana.*
  Even though we claim that justice is blind and that there is one justice for all, this adage more closely reflects reality. Those with money get more justice than those without.

- **There's something fishy going on here** – *Aquí hay gato encerrado.*
  This idiomatic expression has nothing to do with fish. It's meaning is that something suspicious, or out of the ordinary, is happening.

- **They are like two peas in a pod** – *Se junta el hambre con las ganas de comer.*
  This expression is a "folksy" way of saying that two things, or two people, are very similar or bear a close resemblance to one another.

- **Things never seem so bad after a good meal** – *Con pan y vino se anda el camino.*
  This observation states that a full stomach can helps us feel less worried.

- **Time and tides wait for no man** – *Camarón que se duerme, se lo lleva la corriente.*
This proverb uses the concept of the inexorable forward march of time and the inevitable rising and falling of the ocean tides. This proverb means that the best time to do anything is now.

- **Time is gold** – *El tiempo perdido los santos lo lloran.*
Certainly less poetic than its Spanish equivalent, this short adage is no less true, as is the case with the synonymous and more modern phrase, "Time is money." This expression implies that one's time is a valuable commodity and it should not be wasted.

- **Time must take its course** – *No por mucho madrugar amanece más temprano.*
The concept of time is relied upon in this saying to make the point that everything is accomplished in its own due time.

- **To be a dog in the manger** – *Ni raja ni presta el hacha.*
This saying refers to people who do not do a job that needs to be done, and who keep others from doing it, as well. This expression refers to Aesop's fable about a dog that prevents the horse from eating fodder, which the dog won't eat himself.

- **To be a horse of a different color** – *Ser harina de otro costal.*
This expression states that one can't ascribe the same value to two different things just because they are similar.

- **To be driven from pillar to post** – *Ir de la Ceca a la Meca.*
This saying is used to refer to someone who goes here and there, from place to place, in search of something.

- **To be hoisted by one's own petard** – *Vino por lana y salió trasquilado.*
  Ir por lana y volver trasquilado.
The rather antiquated vocabulary on this metaphorical saying means to be caught in a difficult situation for which one is responsible. A "petard" is an explosive device, and "To be hoisted" is to be lifted. Literally translated it means, to be blown up by one's own bomb.

- **To be just what the doctor ordered** – *Caer como pedrada en ojo tuerto.*
This expression refers to something that is exactly the right solution to a problem.

- **To be three sheets to the wind** – *Estar como una cuba*
This saying refers to a person being very drunk. It alludes to the effect on a sailing ship of having three of the ropes (sheets) that hold the sail taught go slack (in the wind), causing the sail to flap and making the ship stagger like drunkard.

- **To be up to one's neck** – *Estar con el agua al cuello.*
This idiom refers to being in trouble or to be deeply involved in some unpleasant business.

- **To each his own** – *Cada loco con su tema.*
This is a short expression that tells us that everyone has their individual likes, dislikes and values.

- **To each his own, and God watching over everyone** – *Cada uno en su casa, y Dios en la de todos.*
This proverb tells us that we are all different, but that God takes care of all of us equally.

- **To err is human, to forgive divine** – *El que tiene boca se equivoca.*
From *"An Essay on Criticism"* by Alexander Pope, this saying tells us that we commit sins and God forgives us. By forgiving others for their mistakes we are doing as God would have us do.

- **To fall on deaf ears** – *A palabras necias, oídos sordos.*
This idiomatic expression refers to talking to people who ignore, disregard and refuse to listen to the one speaking.

- **To fight tooth and nail** – *Defenderse a capa y espada.*
This idiom means to fight violently, with total commitment, to the very end in order to defend or protect something we want, or in which we believe.

To go from pillar to post – *Andar de Herodes a Pilato.*
This expression was used to refer to the game of court tennis and how the ball was banged about. It now refers to going from one place to another, back and forth.

To hit and run – *Tirar la piedra y esconder la mano.*
This expression is often seen as the description of the activities of guerrilla fighters who attack by surprise, or ambush and then disappear. This expression is also used figuratively for the tactics that some people employ in an argument.

To let the fox in the hen house – *Meter el lobo en el redil.*
With obvious origins in the agricultural past, this metaphorical saying is used to describe an unethical person who is supposedly the impartial protector of other people, but whose true interests lie elsewhere.

To promise the moon and stars – *Prometer el oro y el moro.*
   Prometer el cielo y la tierra
This saying or phrase is used to express an exaggerated offer made to convince someone to do something.

To put the cart before the horse – *Empezar la casa por el tejado.*
   Ensillar antes de traer las bestias.
This saying refers to people who reverse the correct order of things, or events. This old expression had its roots in agriculture, when carts and horses were used for transportation.

To sell a pig in a poke – *Dar gato por liebre.*
   Meter gato por liebre.
The original meaning came from a time when people went to market and brought their groceries home in a bag known as a poke. This saying means that the seller cheated the buyer by giving him something different than what was agreed upon in the sale.

To smell a rat – *Aquí hay gato encerrado.*
This saying indicates that something suspicious or unclear is occurring.

- **To split hairs** – *Buscarle cinco patas al gato.*
  This metaphoric idiom refers to people who argue extensively about something trivial and of no real importance.

- **To throw the baby out with the bath water** – *Tirar las frutas frescas con las pochas.*
  This expression warns us not to discard something valuable along with something we don't want.

- **Too little, too late** – *Cuando la partera vino ya el muchacho cargaba leña.*
  This expression is used for any occasion that refers to a late, inadequate response. In the 1900's, this saying was applied to the late arrival of insufficient reinforcements and supplies in the military.

- **Too many cooks spoil the broth** – *Tantas manos en el plato huelen a caca de gato.*
  This expression means that too many people giving directions can ruin a situation.

- **Try to strike a happy medium** – *Ni mucha luz al santo que lo queme, ni poca que no lo alumbre.*
  Ni tan adentro que te quemes, ni tan afuera que te hieles.
  This saying warns us not to exaggerate and try to find a midway point between two extremes.

- **Two heads are better than one** – *Cuatro ojos ven más que dos.*
  This expression says that sometimes a second opinion helps a lot. A person not directly involved in a problem is in a better position to find an objective solution.

NOTES:_____

_____

_____

U

Unwelcome as a fly in the soup – *Quedó como mosca en leche.*
This saying sometimes is used to indicate that a person doesn't
belong in a certain place due to his appearances, or the way he
behaves.

_____

NOTES:_____

_____

_____

V

- **Variety is the spice of life** – *Pan con pan, comida de tontos.*
  This saying explains that change can be very good for people and can add quality to one's life. Adding a little "spice" in one's life makes it better and more interesting.

- **Vent one's spleen** – *Desahogar la ira.*
  The spleen was once considered an organ which caused ill humor and melancholy, therefore, to vent one's spleen meant to release these feelings.

NOTES:_____

_____

_____

W

We all judge others by our own standards – *El ladrón juzga por su condición.*
El león cree que todos son de su condición.
While not as colorful as the Spanish version, the observation, nevertheless, seems to be true. This expression indicates that almost everyone expects that others should act and behave as they expect them to do.

We are all God's creatures – *Al erizo, Dios lo hizo.*
This truism is most often invoked to emphasize that we are all equal and deserve each other's respect.

We don't always get what we want in this life – *Al pobre y al feo todo se le va en deseo.*
This saying points out what most of us know by intuition and experience. This saying means that life does not always give us what we want, but many times we get what we deserve.

What is bred in the bone will come out in the flesh – *La cabra siempre tira al monte.*
This saying makes us understand that people act in accordance with their heritage and upbringing. It is frequently used to disparage the social level of another.

When in Rome, do as the Romans do – *A la tierra que fueres, haz lo que vieres.*
This proverb tells us that we should respect the customs and traditions of wherever we are without attempting to impose our own values.

When it rains, it pours – *Si por allá llueve por aquí no escampa.*
This new version of the British saying "It never rains but it pours" reminds us that when problems appear, they come in overwhelming amounts. It may come from a 1726 book by Jonathan Swift entitled "It cannot rain but it pours."

- **When one door closes, another always opens** – *Cuando una puerta se cierra, otra se abre.*
  This maxim is meant to encourage one who has suffered a failure, or loss, by offering the idea that in life there are always new opportunities waiting in the future.

- **When the cat's away the mice will play** – *Cuando el gato no está, los ratones hacen fiesta.*
  This very common proverb alludes to the propensity of children, workers and people in general to not remain dedicated to a task if they are not supervised.

- **Where there is a will, there is a way** – *Querer es poder.*
  This truism is meant to encourage us to accomplish a goal if by no other means than by the sheer force of will.

- **Where there is smoke, there is fire** – *Cuando el río suena, piedras lleva.*
  As Agatha Christie's Miss Jane Marple would say, "How often gossip is true…That's why people are so interested in it." This expression means that there is always some truth in every rumor.

- **Words are not binding** – *Las palabras se las lleva el viento.*
  This short expression is meant to warn us that any agreement should be reduced to writing in order to make it valid.

NOTES:_____

_____

_____

Y

You cannot be in two places at once – *No se puede repicar, decir misa y andar en la procesión.*
This saying is literally true. One cannot physically be in two places at once.

You can't have your cake and eat it too – *No se puede tener pan y pedazo.*
This saying is often used with reference to a greedy person who wants more that its fair share. In the literal sense, it means that if you cut out a piece of cake and eat it, you cannot longer expect that the cake will still be whole.

You can't make a silk purse out of a sow's ear – *La mona aunque la vistan de seda, mona se queda.*
  Aunque la mona se vista de seda, mona se queda.
  Aunque el marrano sea blanco, lo maten en la villa y
  lo salen con azúcar, siempre es negra la morcilla.
The literal meaning of this proverb is that you cannot make a good product if you start with poor quality materials. It is often applied to the impossibility of changing a person's bad character traits into something more admirable.

You can't teach an old dog new tricks – *Loro viejo no aprende a hablar.*
Over time our habits become ingrained and we get into the rut of living. This saying expresses the common belief that once we are old we cannot change or learn new things. Perhaps if we learn new things our whole life, we can continue to learn when we get old.

You can't judge a book by its cover – *Hay cosas que colgadas parecen bolsas.*
This maxim warns us that appearances do not really tell the truth about what someone is really like.

- **You dig your grave with your teeth** – *De baños, purgas y cenas están las sepulturas llenas.*
  People have known for a long time that certain activities are harmful to your health. In particular, as we know today, overeating will shorten your life.

- **You had better get your act together** – *¡Fíate de la Virgen y no corras!*
  This modern day admonishment simply means that one needs to get organized and to start in order to finish any task.

- **You have to blow your own horn** – *No tener abuela que le cante.*
  Shakespeare, in Much Ado About Nothing says it is, "…most expedient for the wise… to be the trumpet of his own virtues", meaning that one must boast of his own accomplishments for no one else will.

- **You may know by a handful, the whole sack** – *Para la muestra un botón.*
  This proverb no doubt goes back to the days when grains and other products were traded in large bags. The buyer needing to know what he was getting, would take a sample from each lot and thus judge its quality. It is now used to imply that a portion of any thing can tell us about the whole.

- **You shouldn't push your luck** – *Tanto va el cántaro al agua que al fin se rompe.*
  This saying reminds us that over confidence in one's good fortune can often risk disaster.

NOTES:_____

_____

_____

Spanish into English

A

A caballo regalado no se le mira el colmillo – *Never look a gift horse in the mouth.*
Las cosas que nada cuestan se deben recibir sin inconvenientes, aunque tengan algún defecto. Es un refrán que alude a la costumbre que tienen los ganaderos de examinar cuidadosamente la dentadura de los caballos antes de comprarlos para así poder comprobar su edad.

A cada puerco se le llega su San Martín – *Everyone gets their just deserts.*
En la fiesta de San Martín el 11 de noviembre acostumbran matar un cerdo, así que este refrán hace alusión a las personas que viven y hacen el mal y por lo tanto algún día pagarán por sus acciones.

A Dios rogando y con el mazo dando – *Put your faith in God and keep your powder dry.*
  God helps those who help themselves.
Hay que hacer de nuestra parte todo lo que sea posible para lograr lo que deseamos sin esperar que alguien más lo haga o que Dios haga un milagro.

A dónde va el buey que no are – *There is no rest for the wicked.*
Este refrán se refería a que no importaba a donde fuera el pobre, siempre tenía que trabajar. Hasta cierto punto todavía significa lo mismo, pero ahora se usa más en el sentido de que no importa dónde, en todas partes se sufre.

A falta de pan, buenas son tortas – *Half a loaf is better than none.*
Cuando no encuentra lo que quiere, debe resignarse con lo que encuentre.

A la ocasión la pintan calva – *Make hay while the sun shines.*
Este refrán recomienda aprovechar las oportunidades ya que tal vez no se vuelvan a presentar. Este refrán es bastante viejo y tiene su historia con los romanos y una diosa llamada Ocasión.

- **A la tierra que fueres, haz lo que vieres** – *When in Rome, do as the Romans do.*
Es un refrán que nos indica que debemos respetar y portarnos conforme a los usos y costumbres del lugar en que nos hallamos sin tratar de imponer nuestras propias costumbres.

- **A lo hecho, pecho** – *It is no use crying over spilt milk. Stand up, and take your medicine.*
Este refrán se refiere al valor que hay que tener para asumir las consecuencias de los errores cometidos y que ya no tienen remedio.

- **A los bobos se les aparace la Virgen** – *Fortune is wasted on fools.*
Indica este refrán que la buena fortuna favorece a los más incautos.

- **A otro perro con ese hueso** – *Tell it to the Marines. Don't give me that!*
Se usa para rechazar algo que, malo o engañoso, causa enojo.

- **A palabras necias, oídos sordos** – *To fall on deaf ears.*
Este refrán por lo general se usa para responder a insultos y vituperios, pero también cuando las personas hablan y hablan y no dicen nada.

- **Aprendiz de mucho, maestro de nada** – *Jack of all trades, master of none.*
Advierte este refrán que la persona que tiene muchos oficios no logra hacer ninguno bien.

- **A quien madruga Dios le ayuda** – *The early bird gets the worm.*
Hay varias versiones de este mismo refrán. Indica que no se debe ser perezoso. La pereza no da buenos resultados y es un vicio que no goza de buena fama.

- **Agarrarlo con las manos en la masa** – *He was caught red-handed.*
Este refrán se usa para indicar que han sorprendido a una persona haciendo lo que no debía.

Agua pasada no mueve molino – *It's no use crying over spilt milk.*
Aconseja mirar adelante y olvidar el pasado. Se usa generalmente para criticar lo ya pasado y desagradable que no sirve para solucionar ningún problema actual.

Agua que no has de beber, déjala correr – *Keep your nose out of other people's business.*
Si no está interesado en algo, déjalo, otros lo apreciarán o a otros les servirá.

Algo tendrá el agua cuando la bendicen – *There must be something about him/her.*
   There must be something in it.
Este refrán dice que la alabanza sin medida y sin motivo de una persona o cosa, muchas veces es indicio de la existencia de defectos o culpas.

¿Al alcalde, quién lo ronda?– *Might makes right.*
Se usa para ponderar la inmunidad de que gozan las personas que tienen más autoridad.

Al buen entendedor pocas palabras le bastan – *A word to the wise is sufficient.*
Una persona inteligente comprende enseguida lo que se le quiere decir y por lo tanto no necesita muchas explicaciones. Este refrán data de la época de Cervantes en Don Quijote y también se puede encontrar en La Celestina de Fernando de Rojas.

Al César lo que es del César y a Dios lo que es de Dios –
Render unto Caesar that which is Caesar's and unto God that which is God's.
Aconseja que a la gente se le debe dar lo que justamente le corresponde. Este refrán tiene origen en un pasaje de la Biblia cuando los fariseos le preguntan a Jesús si deben pagar tributo a los romanos.

- **Al erizo, Dios lo hizo** – *We are all God's creatures.*
Dice que debemos respetar a todas las personas pese a sus defectos y que no se debe despreciar a nadie ya que todas las criaturas poseen una cualidad provechosa.

- **Al mal tiempo buena cara** – *Keep a stiff upper lip.*
Significa que una persona debe enfrentarse con ánimo y buena disposición a los problemas y las dificultades que se presentan en la vida.

- **Al mejor panadero se le quema el pan** – *Bad things happen in the best of families.*
Se utiliza para expresar que incluso los más hábiles y expertos en cualquier rama o profesión se equivocan y pueden cometer errores.

- **Al mejor cazador se le va la liebre** – *Bad things happen in the best of families.*
Se utiliza para expresar que incluso los más hábiles y expertos en cualquier rama o profesión se equivocan y pueden cometer errores.

- **Al pan, pan y al vino, vino** – *To call a spade a spade.*
En sentido figurado este refrán se usa para pedirle a alguien que hable sin rodeos, y que diga las cosas francamente y con claridad.

- **Al pobre y al feo todo se le va en deseo** – *We don´t always get what we want in this life.*
Este refrán indica que las personas faltas de bienes de fortuna, de ingenio o de apariencia física no pueden lograr salir adelante y lucir ante los demás, o les es más difícil.

- **Al que le caiga el guante que se lo plante** – *If the shoe fits, wear it.*
Este refrán, prácticamente nuevo, indica que una persona sólo se debe aceptar cualquier comentario hecho, si dicho comentario le atañe a esa persona.

Al que no quiere caldo se le dan dos tazas – *Things have a way of turning out just the way you do not want them to.*
Suele usarse para cuando una persona se ve forzada a hacer lo que no quiere y ha rechazado y se jacta de que nunca lo hará. También se usa para obligar a otra persona a hacer algo que no quiere hacer y rechaza hacerlo.

Al que se le come el pan se le reza el padrenuestro – *Never bite the hand that feeds you.*
Este refrán indica que cuando una persona recibe favores de otra persona o le trabaja a alguien, tiene que respetar a esa persona y hacer lo que se le ordene que haga.

Amor con amor se paga – *One good turn deserves another. An eye for an eye, and a tooth for a tooth.*
Este refrán se puede tomar en dos formas, la primera traducción indica que si se hace algo bueno, se puede esperar algo bueno en recompensa. La segunda es una forma sarcástica que implica venganza.

Ande yo caliente, y ríase la gente – *I dress for comfort, not for other people.*
Este refrán se refiere a la gente que da más importancia al bienestar y a la comodidad que a las apariencias.

Antes de que te cases, mira lo que haces – *Look before you leap.*
En sentido literal, aconseja pensar y reflexionar en tan decisivo acto. En general aconseja pensar bien que cualquier asunto grave con el que uno se vaya a enfrentar. Este refrán data de la Edad Media. El marqués de Santanilla lo escribió de la siguiente manera: **Antes que cases, cata que haces, que no es ñudo que así desates**.

Aquí hay gato encerrado – *There's something fishy going on here. I smell a rat.*
Se usa este refrán para indicar que hay sospechas de que alguna cuestión no está muy clara.

- **Árbol que nace torcido jamás su tronco endereza** – *As the twig is bent, so grows the tree.*
  Con este refrán damos a entender que si no se le enseña y se le da buen ejemplo a un niño desde que nace, nunca llegará a ser una persona honesta y buena ya que las costumbres de la niñez perduran hasta la vejez.

- **Arreboles al oriente, aguas al día siguiente** – *Red sun at night, sailors delight; red sun at morning, sailors take warning.*
  Este refrán señala la relación directa que los agricultores encontraban en estos dos fenómenos naturales y que les ayudaba a predecir el tiempo.

- **Arrieros somos y en el camino nos encontramos** – *Be good to everyone on your way up, because you never know whom you will meet on your way down.*
  Este refrán advierte que si se niega un favor a otro, tal vez en el futuro esa persona se desquite negándole algo a esa otra persona.

- **Arrimarse al sol que más calienta** – *To get on the winning side. To jump on the bandwagon.*
  Se refiere este refrán a las personas que buscan únicamente la compañía de personas importantes porque saben que les va a beneficiar estar en su compañía.

- **Aténgase a la Virgen y no corra** – *You'd better get your act together.*
  Indica que no las personas no deben confiar en la ayuda de los demás, sino que deben valerse de sí mismos para obtener lo que desean. Otra variación de este refrán dice: ¡Fíate de la Virgen y no corras!

- **Aunque la mona se vista de seda, mona se queda** – *You can´t make a silk purse out of a sow's ear.*
  Con este refrán se quiere dar a entender que es inútil tratar de aparentar la verdadera índole ya que ésta se delata de todos modos. Se usa más refiriéndose a las personas, pero también se puede usar para cosas.

- **Aunque el marrano sea blanco, lo maten en la villa y lo salen con azúcar, siempre es negra la morcilla.** – *You can't make a silk purse out of a sow's ear.*
Este refrán es igual al anterior, "Aunque la mona se vista de seda, mona se queda." Es decir que es inútil tratar de disfrazar la realidad, porque esta sale a relucir de todas formas.

- **Ayúdate que yo te ayudaré, dijo Dios** – *God helps those who help themselves.*
Este refrán nos enseña que debemos trabajar fuerte para lograr lo que queremos, pues las cosas no van a llegar por arte de gracia con sólo rezar y pedirle ayuda a Dios.

APUNTES:_____

_____

_____

B

- **Barriga llena, corazón contento** – *A full stomach makes for a happy heart.*
  Dice de la satisfacción que se siente de haber comido bien. Aviva la gratitud devocional.

- **Bicho malo nunca muere** – *Bad pennies always turn up.*
  Este refrán se refiere a que lo malo suele durar por mucho tiempo. Hace alusión a aquellas personas que a pesar de ser malas siempre gozan de buena salud.

- **Bueno es culantro pero no tanto** – *Enough is enough.*
  That's going a bit far.
  Indica que el abuso, aunque sea de cosas buenas puede ser dañoso.

- **Buscar una aguja en un pajal** – *Looking for a needle in a hay stack.*
  Se refiere a cuando uno busca algo importante o bueno y nunca lo va a encontrar bien sea porque no existe o porque es muy difícil.

- **Buscarle tres pies al gato** – *To split hairs.*
  Alude a las personas demasiado minuciosas y temáticas que complican las cosas en las que intervienen.

APUNTES:_____

_____

_____

C

- **Caballo grande, ande o no ande** – *Bigger is always better.*
  Este refrán se refiere a las personas que carecen de virtudes pero
  que son de elevada estatura y debido a esta condición pueden
  obtener ciertas ventajas.

- **Cada cabeza es un mundo** – *To each his own.*
  Este refrán mexicano se refiere a la gente que siempre habla de su
  empleo o profesión o a reiteradas alusiones que hace la persona en
  cuanto a sus intereses o preocupaciones.

- **Cada cual es libre de hacer de su capa un sayo** – *To do as one
  pleases.*
  Habla de la libertad que tiene cada persona para obrar según su
  propio albedrío, sin considerar la opinión de los demás.

- **Cada loco con su tema** – *To each his own.*
  Este refrán se aplica con mucha frecuencia a la gente que siempre
  habla de su empleo o profesión o a reiteradas alusiones que hace
  la persona en cuanto a sus intereses o preocupaciones

- **Cada oveja con su pareja** – *Every Jack has his Jill.*
  Birds of a feather flock together.
  Este antiguo refrán se refiere a que debemos escoger nuestras
  amistades y compañías de nuestro mismo rango y nivel social. No
  deben ser ni superiores ni inferiores a lo que somos.

- **Cada uno cuenta de la feria según le va en ella** – *Everyone sees
  things from his own point of view.*
  Este refrán se encuentra en el *Refranero* del marqués de Santillana
  y da a entender que cada persona habla de las cosas según el
  provecho o daño que haya sacado de ella.

- **Cada uno en su casa, y Dios en la de todos** – *Each to his own, and God watching over everyone.*
  Este refrán tiene dos significados. El primero advierte que, por el bien de todos, no es conveniente que todos los miembros de una familia (desde los abuelos hasta los nietos) vivan en la misma casa. El segundo da a entender que nadie debe meterse en los asuntos ajenos.

- **Cada uno es libre de hacer de su culo un candelero** – *To do as one pleases.*
  Es una forma más vulgar de expresar la libertad que tiene cada persona para obrar como bien le plazca sin tener en cuenta la opinión de los demás.

- **Caer como pedrada en ojo tuerto** – *To be just what the doctor ordered.*
  Alude este refrán a que ciertas cosas coinciden o encajan exactamente con otras.

- **Camarón que se duerme, se lo lleva la corriente** – *Time and tide wait for no man.*
  Este refrán le dice a la gente que debe ser diligente y al mismo tiempo los previene del peligro que causa la indolencia.

- **Cargar leña al monte** – *Like coal to Newcastle.*
  Enseña este refrán que es una tontería llevar cosas donde las hay por abundancia.

- **Caridad con trompeta, no me peta (no me agrada)** – *Don't pat yourself on the back.*
  Este refrán critica a los que hacen ostentación de su generosidad y del bien que hacen a otros. Un refrán del Siglo XIX dice: **Ese hace la caridad con reflector**.

- **Cobra fama y échate a dormir** – *Give a dog a bad name.*
  Dice que así como la mala fama es tan difícil de restaurar, la buena fama puede con todo, aunque la evidencia sea otra.

- **Come, calla y no preguntes de dónde sale** – *Mind your own business.*
  Es un refrán que indica que debemos oír, callar y no averiguar lo que no es de nuestra incumbencia.

- **Como cordero al matadero** – *Like leading lambs to the slaughter.*
  Este refrán se refiere al inocente que se deja llevar fácilmente, sin darse cuenta del peligro que le espera.

- **Como no ha aprendido a ser señora se resbala del cojín** – *Breeding will out.*
  Este dicho se refiere a las personas que aparentan ser lo que no son y no saben comportarse en público.

- **Con buen hambre no hay mal pan** – *Beggars can't be choosers.*
  Este refrán recuerda que cuando se está necesitado, cualquier cosa se acepta.

- **Con la vara con que midas, serás medido** – *As you judge, so shall you be judged.*
  Indica que tal como juzguemos a una persona así podemos ser juzgados también.

- **Con pan y vino se anda el camino** – *Things never seem so bad after a good meal.*
  Indica este refrán que debemos cuidar del sustento de las personas que trabajan, si se quiere que cumplan con sus obligaciones y hagan buen trabajo.

- **Confundir el culo con las témporas** – *To not know the difference between his ass and a hole in the ground.*
  Expresión que se usa en frases con las que se comenta que alguien compara o relaciona cosas en realidad muy diferentes o inconexas.

- **Contra viento y marea** – *Come hell or high water.*
  Este refrán se refiere a que se puede lograr alguna cosa pase lo que pase.

- **Cría cuervos y te sacarán los ojos** – *Don't bite the hand that feeds you.*
Es una expresión de desengaño, se refiere a la ingratitud de las personas después de habérseles tratado bien.

- **Cría fama y échate a dormir** – *Give a dog a bad name.*
Dice que así como la mala fama es tan difícil de restaurar, la buena fama puede con todo, aunque la evidencia sea otra.

- **Cuando el gato no está, los ratones hacen fiesta** – *When the cat's away, the mice will play.*
Este refrán indica que cuando la persona en autoridad no está, los subalternos no hacen el trabajo como debe ser. Alude a la falta de responsabilidad de algunas personas cuando se encuentran solas.

- **Cuando el río suena piedras lleva** – *Where there is smoke, there is fire.*
Es un refrán que indica que hay la posibilidad que un rumor pueda ser cierto.

- **Cuando la partera vino ya el muchacho cargaba leña** – *It is too little, too late.*
Se refiere a que muchas veces los favores que se piden llegan demasiado tarde.

- **Cuando una puerta se cierra otra se abre** – *When one door closes, another always opens.*
Se usa este refrán para dar consuelo y ánimo a una persona cuando ha perdido el trabajo o le ha llegado la mala suerte.

- **Cuatro ojos ven más que dos** – *Two heads are better than one.*
Se usa este refrán para dar a entender que los asuntos atendidos cuidadosamente por varias personas pueden tener mejor resultado.

APUNTES:_____

_____

_____

D

- **Dar gato por liebre (Meter gato por liebre)** – *To sell a pig in a poke.*
  Este refrán se suele usar cuando han engañado a una persona en un negocio.

- **Dar una en el clavo y ciento en la herradura** – *To be wrong nine times out of ten.*
  Hace referencia a las malas decisiones que suele hacer la gente y lo difícil que es dar con la verdad.

- **Darle la mano y tomarse hasta el codo** – *Give him an inch, and he will take a mile.*
  Hay ciertas personas que se aprovechan de la bondad de otros y abusan de ella.

- **De baños purgas y cenas están las sepulturas llenas** – *You dig your grave with your teth.*
  Dice que la gente siempre ha creído que ciertas actividades pueden ser mortales, por ejemplo bañarse después de una comida opulenta. Hoy en día la ciencia ha comprobado que una actividad tal como comer demasiado puede acortar la vida.

- **De buenas intenciones está empedrado el infierno** – *The road to hell is paved with good intentions.*
  Explica que los buenos propósitos resultan estériles si no se ponen en práctica.

- **De capa y espada** – *Cloak and dagger*
  Esta expresión data del Siglo XVI y describe unas comedia de Lope de Vega y Calderon de la Barca, las cuales trataban mucho de espias, peleas y aventuras y en las cuales el actor llevaba puesta una capa y normalmente bajo ella ocultaba un espada o daga. Hoy en día la expresión se refiere a la intriga dramática de operativos secretos.

- **De grano en grano llena la gallina el buche** – *Many a mickle makes a muckle.*
  Every little bit helps.
  Se usa para indicar que mediante el ahorro módico pero tenaz se alcanza la riqueza. También se usa para dar a entender que con paciencia y de a poco se pueden alcanzar grandes cosas.

- **De la carrera no queda sino el cansancio** – *Haste makes waste.*
  Da a entender que con hacer las cosas de prisa no se gana nada y sí pueden salir mal. Es mejor con calma y sin afán.

- **De la mano a la boca, se pierde la sopa** – *There is many a slip 'twixt the cup and the lip.*
  Advierte que en un instante se puede esfumar toda esperanza de lograr algo.

- **De los males, el menos** – *The lesser of two evils.*
  Es un refrán que nos aconseja que si hay que escoger entre dos cosas malas, se debe elegir la menos mala. También se usa para expresar conformidad cuando ocurre una desgracia y esta resulta menos grave de lo que se esperaba.

- **De tal palo, tal astilla** – *The apple never falls far from the tree.*
  A chip off the old block.
  Con este refrán se da a entender que los hijos suelen tener las mismas características de sus padres, bien sean buenas o malas.

- **De todo hay en la viña del Señor** – *It takes all sorts to make a world.*
  El refrán nos dice que la vida está constituida por los más variados y contradictorios elementos.

- **Defenderse a capa y espada** – *To fight tooth and nail.*
  Este refrán se refiere a la fiereza con que se peleaba y se defendían antiguamente los pueblos haciendo uso de todos los recursos que tuvieran a su alcance.

- **Del afán no queda sino el cansancio** – *Haste makes waste.*
Da a entender que con hacer las cosas de prisa no se gana nada y sí pueden salir mal. Es mejor con calma y sin afán.

- **Del agua mansa líbrame Dios que de la brava me libraré yo** – *Still waters run deep.*
Este refrán dice que se debe cuidar de las personas que disfrazan sus intenciones con dulzura y bondad mientras es más fácil confiar en la persona que dice lo que piensa.

- **Del árbol caído todos hacen leña** – *A fallen man is everybody's prey.*
Denota lo fácil que es abusar y aprovecharse de las personas que caen en desgracia y no pueden defenderse.

- **Del dicho al hecho hay mucho trecho** – *It is easier said than done. There is many a slip betwixt cup and lip.*
Se refiere a que es más fácil prometer que cumplir y por lo tanto no se debe confiar en las promesas.

- **Del plato a la boca se enfría la sopa** – *There is many a slip 'twixt the cup and the lip.*
Advierte que en un instante se puede esfumar toda esperanza de lograr algo.

- **Dígale cotudo, antes de que él se lo diga** – *Strike while the iron is hot.*
Este refrán indica que debemos aprovechar el momento para decir o hacer lo que pensamos antes de que otro se adelante y lo haga, perdiendo así nuestra oportunidad.

- **Dime con quién andas y te diré quién eres** – *A man is known by the company he keeps.*
En un sentido general este refrán dice que por las amistades que tiene una persona se pueden deducir sus gustos y comportamiento.

- **Dios aprieta pero no ahoga** – *God never gives us more than we can handle.*
  God tempers the wind to the unshorn lamb.
  Dice que no se debe desconfiar de la misericordia Divina. Tal vez se sufra un poco pero para todo hay solución.

- **Dios da la llaga, pero da la medicina** – *The hand that gave the wound must give the cure.*
  Dice que por lo general el remedio a los sufrimientos comunes se encuentra en la misma persona que los causa.

- **Dios le da pan a quien no tiene dientes** – *It is an unfair world.*
  Life isn't fair.
  El refrán original que se encuentra en *La Celestina* decía **Dio Dios habas a quien no tiene quijadas.** Los dos refranes se refieren a la fortuna o buena suerte que le llega a la persona menos indicada para disfrutarla.

- **Dios los cría y ellos se juntan** – *Birds of a feather flock together.*
  Este refrán hace comentario referente la unión o amistad entre personas que comparten una afición, una forma de vida o un mismo vicio.

- **Donde no hay harina, todo es mohína** – *Poverty breeds discontent.*
  Este refrán indica que la pobreza y la necesidad suelen ser causa de disgustos y descontentos. Este refrán es bastante antiguo, ya que el marqués de Santillana lo citaba en otra forma, **Mohína es la casa que no ha harina.**

- **Donde quiera hay faldriquera teniendo las naguas rotas** – *It's the same the whole world over.*
  Este refrán indica que cuando la persona es pobre tiene que someterse a lo que encuentre porque en todas partes va a ser igual.

- **Donde quiera se cuecen habas** – *It's the same the whole world over.*
  Indica este refrán que las debilidades humanas existen en todas partes y nadie es inmune a ellas.

APUNTES:_____

_____

_____

E

- **Echando a pique se aprende** – *Failure is the best teacher.*
  Practice makes perfect.
  Este refrán indica que para poder obtener dominio completo de una
  profesión hay que pasar por un período inicial de desaciertos.

- **El buey suelto bien se lame** – *There is nothing like freedom.*
  Se refiere al goce de la libertad y las ventajas de la autosuficiencia.

- **El comer y el rascar el trabajo es comenzar** – *The hardest part of
  any job is getting started.*
  The first step in any journey is always the most difficult.
  Este refrán tiene dos aplicaciones. Una es animar a las personas a
  que empiecen a hacer algo que no quieren hacer. La segunda, en
  un sentido más general indica que lo difícil de un trabajo sólo está
  en comenzarlo.

- **El cura predica pero no aplica** – *Practice what you preach.*
  Este refrán indica que debemos poner atención a las
  amonestaciones y a las enseñanzas orales, sin parar a pensar si la
  persona que las enseña las está poniendo en práctica o no.

- **El hábito no hace al monje** – *The clothes don´t make the man.*
  Este refrán nos enseña que no debemos juzgar a las personas por
  su apariencia física, ya que las apariencias engañan.

- **El hombre propone y Dios dispone** – *Man proposes and God
  disposes.*
  Un refrán que enseña que el logro de nuestras determinaciones
  depende de la voluntad de Dios. También se usa cuando en un
  negocio surge un obstáculo inesperado que da al traste con todo.

- **El ladrón juzga por su condición** – *We all judge others by our
  own standards.*
  Este refrán indica que las personas suelen juzgar a los demás de
  acuerdo a lo que son ellos mismos.

- **El león cree que todos son de su condición** – *We all judge others by our own standards.*
Este refrán indica que las personas suelen juzgar a los demás de acuerdo a lo que son ellos mismos.

- **El mismo perro con distinto collar** – *The same music with a different tune.*
Se aplica generalmente esta expresión a los políticos. En general indica que a pesar del cambio que se haga, siguen los mismos vicios o el mismo comportamiento.

- **El necio es atrevido y el sabio comedido** – *Fools rush in where angels fear to tread.*
Dice este refrán que la gente tonta y desprevenida se lanza a hacer las cosas sin pensar, mientras lo que bien saben los riesgos no se atreven a aventurar.

- **El ojo del amo engorda el caballo** – *It is the master's eye that makes the mill go.*
Es un refrán que recuerda que es conveniente que el dueño o patrón cuide de sus posesiones o negocios personalmente para obtener buenos resultados.

- **El pez grande se come al chico** – *It's a dog eat dog world.*
The big fish swallows up the little one.
Advierte del poder que tiene el más fuerte y el riesgo que se corre al negociar con entidades de mayor influencia.

- **El que a buen árbol se arrima, buena sombra le cobija** – *It's always useful to have friends in high places.*
Este refrán se encuentra en el *Libro del caballero Zifar* y se refiere a las ventajas que logra la persona que tiene protección de alguien con poder.

- **El que a hierro mata, a hierro muere** – *He who lives by the sword, dies by the sword.*
Advierte este refrán que tarde o temprano seremos víctimas de los mismos daños que hayamos causado a nuestros semejantes.

- **El que calla otorga** – *Silence gives consent.*
  Este refrán señala que la persona que no protesta ni se opone a una idea es porque está de acuerdo con ella.

- **El que con lobos anda a aullar aprende** – *If you lie down with dogs, you are going to get up with fleas.*
  Dice de la influencia tan grande que pueden tener las malas compañías o los malos amigos.

- **El que con niños se acuesta, orinado amanece** – *If you lie down with dogs, you will get up with fleas.*
  Este refrán se refiere a los peligros que corre una persona cuando se asocia o comparte una actividad con personas que no tienen seriedad, experiencia o responsabilidad.

- **El que escupe a lo alto, a la cara le cae** – *Never spit into the wind.*
  Indica que las injurias dirigidas a personas de alto rango en vez de baldonarlas van a ser detrimento para quien las dice. El *Eclesiatés* dice *"El que tire la piedra a lo alto se expone a que le caiga en la cabeza"*.

- **El que esté libre de culpa que tire la primera piedra** – *Let he who is without sin cast the first stone.*
  Este refrán enseña que no debemos criticar ni juzgar a lo demás por sus fallas ya que todos las tenemos. Encontramos este proverbio en el evangelio de San Juan 8:7.

- **El que la hace la paga** – *One must face the music.*
  Este refrán alude a que hay que aceptar responsabilidad por las acciones hechas, así sean buenas o malas.

- **El que mal anda mal acaba** – *You made your bed, now lie in it.*
  Se dice de las personas que tienen malas costumbres y acaban víctimas de éstas. Cómo ha sido la vida así será el fin.

- **El que más madrugó una bolsa de oro se encontró** – *The early bird catches the worm.*
  Este refrán alude a las personas que madrugan a realizar sus trabajos o que los hacen a tiempo y por lo tanto salen premiados.

- **El que menos corre, vuela** – *Slow and steady wins the race.*
Este refrán recuerda que el que es constante, aunque lento hasta el final, lleva la ventaja al que empieza con rapidez y se le agotan los esfuerzos antes de terminar.

- **El que mucho abarca poco aprieta** – *Don't bite off more than you can chew.*
Este refrán se refiere a las personas que se embarcan en muchos proyectos y no los pueden realizar adecuadamente. También a los que quieren todo y por querer más quedan sin nada.

- **El que mucho habla, mucho yerra** – *Least said, soonest mended. The less said, the better.*
Es un refrán muy antiguo que se encuentra en el Libro de buen amor y que dice que la locuacidad lleva a hacer que la persona cometa muchos errores.

- **El que mucho se agachó hasta el culo se le vio** – *If you stoop to low, your ass will show.*
Este refrán indica que la persona que confunde la obediencia con la servidumbre pierde lo más preciado de sí, su dignidad. Ser muy humilde y sumiso puede convertirse en bajeza.

- **El que no arriesga un huevo, no tiene un pollo** – *One cannot make an omelette without breaking some eggs.*
Este refrán enseña que para poder alcanzar las metas deseadas hay que correr ciertos riesgos.

- **El que no llora, no mama** – *The squeaky wheel gets the grease.*
Este refrán aconseja insistir en lo que se pide, si se quiere conseguir un objetivo.

- **El que quiere celeste que le cueste** – *Nothing ventured, nothing gained.*
Este refrán indica que el afán y el deseo de obtener alguna cosa obliga a aguantar los sinsabores, esfuerzos y problemas que suponga el conseguirlos.

- **El que quiera marrones que aguante tirones** – *No pain, no gain.*
  Es un refrán colombiano que indica que el afán y el deseo de obtener algo obliga a aguantar los sinsabores, esfuerzos y problemas que suponga el conseguirlos.

- **El que ríe de último ríe mejor** – *He who laughs last, laughs best.*
  Es un refrán que advierte el peligro de burlarse de otra persona.

- **El que se casa quiere casa y costal para la plaza** – *Married people need a home of their own.*
  Un refrán que aconseja a los recién casados no vivir con la familia bajo el mismo techo, ya que eso se presta para problemas.

- **El que se queja, sus males aleja** – *Misery loves company.*
  Este refrán indica que tener con quien desahogarse es como un sedante.

- **El que se va a Quito, pierde su banquito** – *Finders keepers, losers weepers.*
  El que se fue a Sevilla, perdió su silla – *He who goes to the fair, loses his chair.*
  Indica este refrán que si dejamos el lugar o el trabajo donde estamos, otros vendrán y lo ocuparán.

- **El que siembra vientos recoge tempestades** – *Sow the wind and reap the whirlwind.*
  Es un refrán que advierte las malas consecuencias que resultan de las malas acciones. Como muchos otros refranes, éste fue extraído de las Sagradas Escrituras, más exacto del profeta Oseas 8-7.

- **El que tenga rabo de paja que no se arrime a la candela** – *If you can't take the heat, stay out of the kitchen.*
  Previene a las personas orgullosas o de carácter delicado que no es bueno tratar con bromistas para no exponerse a las chanzas de estos.

- **El tiempo perdido los santos lo lloran** – *Time is gold.*
Advierte que estar de vago y perder el tiempo no es bueno sino que se debe estar siempre ocupado como lo hacían los santos.

- **El que tiene boca, se equivoca** – *To err is human.*
Por lo general se usa este refrán como una excusa cuando se ha dicho algo que no se debería decir. Pero ultimamente se ha agregado una respuesta...**pero el que tiene seso no dice eso**.

- **Empezar la casa por el tejado** – *To put the cart before the horse.*
Este refrán se aplica a las personas impacientes que quieren ver el resultado de una empresa sin antes poner todo el empeño para su eficaz resultado.

- **En arca abierta, el justo peca** – *Everyone has little larceny in his heart.*
Advierte que cuando la ocasión se presenta es tan tentadora que la persona más honesta puede sucumbir y volverse deshonesta. Hay otros refranes que sugieren lo mismo, que no se debe ser descuidado dando así facilidades a otros.

- **En boca cerrada no entra mosca** – *Silence is golden.*
Advierte que se debe ser discreto y la importancia de saber callar a tiempo.

- **En casa de carpintero, puerta de cuero** – *The shoemaker's children go barefoot.*
Este refrán dice que justamente donde hay la facilidad para hacer o tener alguna cosa específica, suele haber falta de ella.

- **En casa de herrero azadón de palo** – *The cobbler's children have no shoes.*
The shoemaker's wife is always worst shod.
Este refrán dice que justamente donde hay la facilidad para hacer o tener alguna cosa específica, suele haber falta de ella.

- **En el peligro se conoce el amigo** – *A friend in need is a friend indeed.*
  Señala que cuando llegan los problemas y la adversidad, se conoce a los verdaderos amigos por la forma como se comportan.

- **En la mesa y en el juego se conoce al caballero** – *Breeding will out.*
  Un refrán muy popular y muy exacto ya que en estos dos terrenos se revela el grado de educación de las personas. Hay otros lugares donde se puede ver la educación de la persona, pero estos dos son inequívocos.

- **En la puerta del horno se quema el pan** – *Anything that can go wrong, will go wrong.*
  Este refrán indica que las cosas pueden cambiar inadvertidamente y al último minuto.

- **En menos que canta un gallo** – *In a flash.*
  Before you can say Jackie Robinson.
  Este refrán indica la rapidez con la que se puede realizar alguna acción o trabajo.

- **En mi casa estoy, rey soy** – *A man's house is his castle.*
  Este refrán dice que el hombre en su casa es el que manda, aunque no lo haga en ningún otro lugar.

- **En río revuelto, ganancia de pescadores** – *It's an ill wind that blows nobody any good.*
  Indica que el desorden y en la guerra suelen ser ocasiones propicias para que otros ganen. En otras palabras, se refiere a las personas que se aprovechan de los males de los demás.

- **En tierra de ciegos, el tuerto es rey** – *In the land of the blind, the one-eyed man is king.*
  Indica que donde no hay sino nulidades, el mediocre se convierte en figura importante.

- **Entre bueyes no hay cornadas** – *There's honor among thieves.*
Expresa la idea que los de la misma índole se respetan por miedo o por ser iguales.

- **Entre ecuestre y pedestre** – *He doesn't know if he is afoot or on horseback.*
Esta expresión se refiere a una persona que, por confundido o indeciso, no sabe que pensar o hacer.

- **Entre gustos no hay disgustos** – *One man's meat is another man's poison.*
Este refrán nos advierte que las cosas que son buenas o que le gustan a una persona, tal vez no sean del agrado de la otra y que por lo tanto debemos respetar los gustos de los demás.

- **En un abrir y cerrar de ojos** – *In a blink of an eye.*
  In two shakes of a lamb's tail.
Aunque no es un refrán, indica que las cosas pueden suceder en un instante.

- **Éramos pocos y parió la abuela** – *Just when we thought things couldn't get worse, they did.*
  That is the last straw.
  When it rains, it pours
Un dicho muy español que indica que cuando estamos en una situación difícil y agobiada, viene a añadirse otra que redobla la gravedad.

- **Escoba nueva barre bien** – *A new broom sweeps the best.*
Muy a menudo este refrán se refiere al cambio de mandato de los políticos. Es decir salir de los viejos corruptos y esperar que los nuevos hagan mejor trabajo.

- **Ese es otro cantar** – *That's another kettle of fish.*
Este refrán enseña que a una cosa no se aplica la misma actitud o consideración que a otra, auque sea parecida.

- **Estar como una cuba** – *To be three sheets to the wind.*
  Este dicho se refiere a una persona que está bien borracha. Una cuba es un barril donde se guarda el vino, así que una persona bien borracha está llena de una bebida alcohólica igual que una cuba.

- **Estar con el agua al cuello** – *To be up to one's neck.*
  Esta expresión indica que nos encontramos en apuros, en una situación grave o difícil.

- **Estar de veinticinco alfileres** – *Dressed to the nines.*
  Dressed to kill.
  Es una expresión con la cual se da a entender que la persona está muy acicalada y bien vestida. Hace alusión a los muchos alfileres que usan las modistas para elaborar con precisión y elegancia los trajes.

APUNTES:_____

_____

_____

G

Gato con guantes no caza ratones – *A cat in mittens catches no mice.*
Enseña lo difícil que es hacer algunas tareas con demasiados miramientos, especialmente para el que no está acostumbrado a ellos.

Gato escaldado del agua fría huye – *Once bitten, twice shy.*
  To be gun shy.
Este refrán advierte que la persona que ha pasado por un rato amargo, en lo sucesivo rehuye todo aquello que se lo recuerde.

Genio y figura hasta la sepultura – *The leopard can't change his spots.*
Este proverbio citado en el libro *Cinco horas con Mario*, de Miguel Delibes, se refiere a las personas inalterables en su carácter, que toda su vida han sido fieles a su forma de ser sin cambiar un ápice.

APUNTES:_____

_____

_____

H

- **Hablando del Rey de Roma y él que asoma** – *Speak of angels and you hear their wings flapping.*
  Esta expresión se usa para comentar que una persona llega justamente el momento en que se alude a ella.

- **Hay cosas que colgadas parecen bolsas** – *You can't tell a book by its cover.*
  En otras palabras, las apariencias engañan.

- **Haz el bien, y no mires a quién** – *Do good and dread no shame.*
  Este refrán enseña que debemos hacer buenas obras en forma desinteresada, sin discriminación ni parcialidad sectaria.

- **Hecha la ley, hecha la trampa** – *Laws are made to be broken.*
  Este aforismo de origen romano *"Inventa lege, inventa fraude"* nos dice que más se tardan en promulgar leyes y normas, que en hallar forma de quebrantarlas, los que están listos a hacerlo.

- **Herradura que mucho suena algún clavo le falta** – *A wolf in sheep's clothing.*
  Este refrán se refiere a la gente que presume de tener cualidades o una posición falsa o inmerecida pero hace mucho alarde de tenerla y merecerla.

- **Hierba mala nunca muere** – *A bad penny always turns up.*
  Only the good die young.
  Este refrán se refiere a que lo malo suele durar por mucho tiempo. Hace alusión a aquellas personas que a pesar de ser malas siempre gozan de buena salud.

- **Hijo de tigre, sale pintado** – *The apple never falls far from the tree.*
  A chip off the old block.
  Con este refrán se da a entender que los hijos suelen tener las mismas características de sus padres, bien sea buenas o malas.

Hombre prevenido vale por dos – *Forewarned is forearmed.*
Elogia a las personas que son previsoras ya que ellas se anticipan
a los problemas y adelantan las soluciones.

Huyendo del trueno, cayó en el relámpago – *Out of the frying
pan, into the fire.*
Este refrán hace referencia a los que por salir de una situación
problemática se meten en otra peor.

APUNTES:_____

_____

_____

I

- **Ir de Herodes a Pilatos** – *Out of the frying pan, into the fire.*
  Este refrán alude a la vida de Jesús que de pequeño se escapó de
  Herodes y más tarde cayó en manos de Pilatos, quien lo mando
  crucificar. Por lo tanto cuando se usa esta expresión indica ir de
  mal en peor.

- **Ir por lana y volver trasquilado** – *To be hoisted by one's own
  petard.*
  Give someone enough rope and they'll hang themselves.
  Alude a la persona incauta que sufre una pérdida en algo que
  esperaba sacar un buen provecho.

- **Ir de la Ceca a la Meca** – *To be driven from pillar to post.*
  Se usa este refrán para referirse a las personas que van de un
  lugar a otro en busca de algo.

APUNTES:_____

_____

_____

L

La avaricia rompe el saco – *A rich man and his money are soon parted.*
Este refrán advierte que por el ansia de obtener más se puede perder el logro de una ganancia moderada.

Ladrón que roba ladrón tiene cien años de perdón – *It's not a crime to steal from a thief.*
Se usa como disculpa relativa a quien comete una mala acción contra otra persona que comete malas acciones.

La cabra siempre tira al monte – *What is bred in the bone will come out in the flesh.*
En un sentido peyorativo da a entender que cada persona actúa de acuerdo a su naturaleza y a la forma como fue criada.

La ignorancia es atrevida – *A little knowledge is a dangerous thing.*
Se dice de las personas que opinan sobre cosas de las cuales no tienen la menor idea o sin pensar, acometen obras peligrosas.

La letra, con sangre entra – *Spare the rod, spoil the child.*
Este viejo refrán tiene dos sentidos, por un lado enseña que el esfuerzo es necesario para el aprendizaje. Por otro lado, era una forma antigua de defender el castigo físico como método pedagógico eficaz.

La ley del embudo: lo ancho para ellos y lo angosto para uno – *One law for one's self, another for everyone else.*
    To be above the law.
La forma como se aplica o se miden las situaciones varía conforme al interés de cada persona. Este refrán indica la falta de equidad y de justicia.

- **La ley es para los de ruana** – *There is one law for the rich and another for the poor.*
  Este refrán colombiano advierte que por más que se diga que la justicia es ciega, muchas veces la ley sólo se aplica a los de menos recursos económicos.

- **La miel no se hizo para la jeta del asno** – *To cast pearls before swine.*
  Critica este refrán a las personas sin gusto ni sensibilidad que rechazan lo bueno por no saber apreciarlo. Aconseja no ofrecer exquisiteces a quien no sabe valorarlas.

- **La mona aunque la vistan de seda, mona se queda** – *You can't make a silk purse out of a sow's ear.*
  Con este refrán se quiere dar a entender que es inútil tratar de aparentar la verdadera índole ya que ésta se delata de todos modos. Se usa más refiriéndose a las personas, pero también se puede usar para cosas.

- **La ocasión hace al ladrón** – *A bad padlock invites a picklock.*
  Advierte que cuando la ocasión se presenta es tan tentadora que la persona más honesta puede sucumbir y volverse deshonesta. Hay otros refranes que sugieren lo mismo, que no se debe ser descuidado dando así facilidades a otros.

- **La ropa sucia se lava en casa** – *Don't wash dirty linens in public.*
  Este refrán aconseja que los problemas entre familia se deben arreglar en la intimidad del hogar sin enterar a los extraños.

- **La sarna con gusto no pica y si pica no mortifica** – *It's up to him/her.*
  Indica que las cosas ocasionadas por decisiones propias y voluntarias no incomodan y tal vez pueden ser hasta agradables.

- **Las palabras se las lleva el viento** – *Words are not binding.*
  Este refrán implica que no se debe siempre confiar en promesas orales, es mejor tenerlas por escrito.

Lo cortés no quita lo valiente – *Politeness is not a sign of weakness.*
Dice este refrán que la educación y los buenos modales no causan ningún problema, todo lo contrario, defienden cualquier convicción o ideal.

Lo que por agua viene, por agua se va – *Easy come, easy go.*
Este refrán colombiano indica que lo que se obtiene sin mayor esfuerzo puede desaparecer de igual manera.

Los caballos viejos se buscan para rascarse – *Birds of a feather flock together.*
Este refrán hace referencia a que los de la misma estirpe se buscan y andan juntos.

Loro viejo, no aprende a hablar – *You can't teach an old dog new tricks.*
Este refrán se refiere al hecho que las personas mayores tienen dificultad en el aprendizaje de alguna ciencia u oficio nuevo.

APUNTES:_____

_____

_____

M

- **Madre pía, daño cría** – *Spare the rod and spoil the child.*
  Este refrán da a entender que la excesiva indulgencia de las madres es prejudicial para los hijos.

- **Mal de muchos, consuelo de todos** – *The same thing happens to a lot of other people.*
  We are all in the same boat.
  Indica que las circunstancias adversas pueden sobrellevarse más fácilmente si afectan a otras personas.

- **Maldición de gallinazo nunca llega al espinazo** – *Sticks and stones may break my bones, but words will never hurt me.*
  Este refrán aconseja despreciar y no hacer caso a los vituperios y maldiciones de la gente ruin. Según la historia, el rey Fernando III no lo entendía así, pues él le temía más a la maldición de las viejas de su reino que a todos los moros que, según él, estaban de la parte de acá del mar y del otro lado del mar. Se refiere a España y a Marruecos.

- **Más sabe el diablo por viejo que por diablo** – *There is nothing like the old horse for the hard road.*
  There's no substitute for experience.
  Señala que los conocimientos más valiosos son aquellos que se adquieren con la experiencia.

- **Más vale lo malo conocido que lo bueno por conocer** – *Better the devil you know than the devil you don't.*
  Dice este refrán que se deben preferir los modestos medios de que se dispone para alcanzar un fin a aquellos que se creen mejores pero que son desconocidos.

- **Más vale llegar a tiempo que ser convidado** – *Better late than never.*
El refrán enseña sobre el don de la oportunidad que es el mejor aliado para lograr cualquier empeño. Tirso de Molina lo decía en otra forma: La ocasión hace al dichoso.

- **Más vale pájaro en mano que ciento volando** – *A bird in the hand is worth two in the bush.*
Este refrán aconseja que dejemos las cosas inseguras y que nos aferremos de las cosas más seguras aunque sean pequeñas o pocas.

- **Más vale prevenir que curar** – *An ounce of prevention is worth a pound of cure.*
Enseña que es preferible tomar las medidas necesarias para conjurar un mal que tenerlo que combatir más tarde.

- **Más vale prevenir que tener que lamentar** – *An ounce of prevention is worth a pound of cure.*
Dice que es mejor prevenir el mal que luego tener que remediarlo. Aunque se refiere a estados físicos, su uso más común es en el sentido figurado.

- **Más vale ser cabeza de ratón que cola de león** – *It is better to reign in Hell than to serve in Heaven.*
Better to be a big fish in a small pond, than a small fry in the ocean.
Se refiere este refrán a que es mejor ser el primero o más importante en una asociación o empresa pequeña, que ser el último en una corporación o empresa grande.

- **Más vale solo que mal acompañado** – *Better to be alone than in bad company.*
Es un refrán que enseña que es preferible estar solo que rodeado de personas que no son de nuestro agrado. En otras palabras, evitar las malas compañías.

- **Más vale tarde que nunca** – *Better late than never.*
Indica que nunca es tarde para hacer aquello que nos trae placer o beneficio.

- **Más vale una vez colorado, que ciento descolorido** – *Better to be embarrassed once than to have regrets forever.*
Indica que es preferible afrontar con firmeza las situaciones difíciles, no importa la vergüenza que se pase. Enseña este refrán que es mejor hacerle frente a la vergüenza, que guardarla en el corazón hasta enfermarlo.

- **Matrimonio y mortaja, del cielo bajan** – *Marriages are made in heaven.*
Este refrán se refiere a la voluntad de Dios o a que el destino así lo determina y por lo tanto no está bajo nuestro control.

- **Muchos son los llamados y pocos los escogidos** – *Many are called, few are chosen.*
Esta frase tomada del Evangelio de San Mateo 22:14, alude al número de los predestinados a la gloria es menor que el de los que cooperan en las obras de Dios. En un sentido más común dice que el número de personas que logran un objetivo es menor que el número que aspira a conseguirlo.

- **Muerto el ahijado, acabado el compadrazgo**
Muerto el perro, se acabó la rabia – *It's better to kill the snake before it bites you.*
Este refrán enseña que la mejor manera de solucionar un problema o acabar con un mal es acabar con el agente que lo causa.

APUNTES:_____

_____

_____

N

Nadie diga, de esta agua no beberé, porque le toca ahogarse en ella – *Never say never.*
Este refrán previene contra las declaraciones categóricas, ya que no sabemos lo que nos depare el futuro y tal vez tengamos que hacer lo que no nos gusta.

Nadie sabe el pan que se amasa en casa, ni la vida que se pasa – *Don't criticize your brother until you have walked a mile in his shoes.*
Este refrán enseña que las apariencias engañan. Nadie sabe las tristezas y tragedias de otros puestos que no viven con ellos.

Nadie sabe la sed con que otro bebe – *No body knows the troubles that others have seen.*
Este refrán enseña que nadie se encuentra en la capacidad de juzgar las necesidades de sus semejantes.

Ni canta ni come fruta – *He's being a dog in the manger.*
Con este refrán nos referimos a las personas que no saben hacer nada, ni tratan, pero creen que lo saben todo.

Ni mucha luz al santo que lo queme, ni poca que no le alumbre – *Try to strike a happy medium.*
Este refrán aconseja la prudencia. Advierte que la intensidad del afecto no debe ser tan vehemente que pueda fastidiar a la otra persona, ni tan disminuido que pueda pasar desapercibido.

Ni raja ni presta el hacha – *He's being a dog in the manger.*
Este refrán colombiano se refiere a las personas egoístas que no hacen las cosas a tiempo ni permiten que otras las hagan.

Ni tan adentro que te quemes, ni tan afuera que te hieles – *Try to strike a happy médium.*
Se refiere a que no se deben exagerar las cosas y llevarlas hasta el extremo.

- **No dejes para mañana lo que puedas hacer hoy** – *Never put off until tomorrow what can be done today.*
Aconseja este refrán la puntualidad en el cumplimiento de las obligaciones.

- **No era nada lo del ojo y lo tenía en la mano** – *There was nothing to it.*
Con este refrán se trata de dar poca importancia a un suceso grave.

- **No hagas mal que esperes bien** – *You reap what you sow.*
Advierte que cuando se hacen malas obras no se debe esperar una recompensa.

- **No hay cuña que más apriete que la del mismo palo** – *Servants make the worst masters.*
Metafóricamente se refiere al hecho de que a veces las personas más allegadas son las más peligrosas o las que más daño nos pueden causar.

- **No hay mal que dure cien años ni cuerpo que lo resista** – *Nothing goes on forever.*
Es un refrán que hasta cierto punto da consuelo al que sufre un contratiempo dando a entender que pronto terminará la mala hora.

- **No hay mal que por bien no venga** – *Every cloud has a silver lining.*
Da a entender que un suceso nefasto a veces es ocasión de otro más venturoso.

- **No hay mejor cirujano que el acuchillado** – *The best cure is the hair of the dog that bit you.*
Es un refrán que da crédito a las personas con experiencia y las elogia considerándolas más aptas para cierto trabajo.

- **No hay miel sin hiel** – *There is no rose without a thorn.*
Este refrán indica que por lo general un acontecimiento favorable llega al tiempo con uno desfavorable.

- **No hay moros en la costa** – *The coast is clear.*
Avisa este refrán que se puede hablar o actuar abiertamente puesto que no hay nadie prestando atención. Este refrán se refiere a la época de la invasión árabe en España.

- **No hay nada tan atrevido como la ignorancia** – *A little knowledge is a dangerous thing.*
Se dice de las personas que opinan sobre cosas de las cuales no tienen la menor idea o no dominan el tema.

- **No hay peor sordo que el que no quiere oír** – *There are none so deaf as those who will not hear.*
Indica que es inútil persuadir a una persona que con tozudez rehúsa aceptar los consejos que se le dan.

- **No hay que ensillar antes de traer las bestias** – *Don't put the cart before the horse.*
Este refrán muy colombiano se aplica a las personas impacientes que quieren ver el resultado sin antes poner todo el empeño para su eficaz resultado.

- **No por mucho madrugar amanece más temprano** – *Time must take its course.*
Es un refrán que aconseja tener paciencia al iniciar una tarea si no se han hecho de antemano los preparativos.

- **No se ganó Zamora en una hora** – *Rome wasn't built in a day.*
Recomienda paciencia antes toda obra de considerable envergadura. Este refrán alude a los siete meses de asedio sufridos por Zamora, en España en el año 1072.

- **No se pescan truchas a bragas enjutas** – *Nothing ventured, nothing gained.*
Este refrán indica que para conseguir algo en la vida hay que correr algunos riesgos.

- **No se puede repicar, decir misa y andar en la procesión** – *You cannot be in two places at once.*
  Advierte que es imposible hacer dos cosas o más a la vez, ni se puede estar en dos sitios al mismo tiempo. Sólo se puede hacer una cosa a la vez.

- **No se puede tener pan y pedazo** – *You can't have your cake and eat it too.*
  Indica que hay personas que por su avaricia quieren más de lo que les corresponde.

- **No siempre está el palo para cucharas, ni la masa para bollos** – *For every time there is a season.*
  The circumstances are not favorable.
  Este refrán colombiano indica que no todas las circunstancias son igualmente favorables: por lo tanto debemos aprovechar las favorables y consolarnos en las adversas.

- **No sólo de pan vive el hombre** – *Man does not live by bread alone.*
  Enseña que el aspecto alimenticio no es lo único que sustenta al ser humano. Se requiere también el alimento espiritual. Este proverbio se encuentra en Deuterios 8:3 y en el Evangelio de San Mateo 4:4.

- **No tener abuela que le cante** – *You have to blow your own horn.*
  Dice este refrán que para figurar o para que le tomen en cuenta las hazañas, a veces hay que alabarse así mismo ya que nadie más lo hará.

- **No todo el monte es orégano** – *Life is not a bowl of cherries.*
  Life is not a bed of roses.
  Enseña este refrán que no todo en la vida es tan sencillo y bello como parece a primera vista.

- **No todo lo que brilla es oro** – *All that glitters is not gold.*
  Con este refrán se trata de prevenir contra las apariencias, que a menudo esconden una realidad no muy buena.

- **Nunca diga de esta agua no beberé, porque le toca ahogarse en ella** – *Never say never.*
  Este refrán previene contra las declaraciones categóricas, ya que no se sabe lo que nos depare el futuro y tal vez tengamos que hacer lo que no nos gusta.

- **Nunca falta un roto para un descosido** – *Birds of a feather flock together.*
  Da a entender que hasta la persona más despreciable encuentra a otra persona de su misma condición.

APUNTES:_____

_____

_____

O

- **Obras son amores y no buenas razones** – *Actions speak louder than words.*
  Aconseja responder a las necesidades ajenas con hechos y no con buenas palabras. También advierte devolver la gratitud no sólo con palabras sino con hechos también.

- **Oficial de mucho, maestro de nada** – *A jack of all trades, but master of none.*
  Con este refrán se alude en forma irónica a los que pretenden saber de todo pero en realidad no saben nada, ni siquiera los elementos básicos.

- **Ojo por ojo y diente por diente** – *An eye for an eye and a tooth for a tooth.*
  Este precepto extraído del libro del *Éxodo* que se ha convertido en refrán apoya la venganza como norma de la justicia.

- **Ojos que no ven corazón que no siente** – *Out of sight, out of mind.*
  Dice que las penas y los sufrimientos se sienten menos si estamos lejos de las personas que las padecen. Santillana en su *Refranero* anota este refrán un poco diferente, dice: **Ojos que no ven, corazón que no quiebra.** Este refrán ha sido combinado con otro "Perro que ladra no muerde" quedando así un nuevo refrán **Ojos que no ven, perro que no ladra** dando a entender que si no vemos lo que ocurre no decimos nada. Usado más en el caso de enamorados, si no ven lo que la otra persona hace, entonces no riñen.

- **Otro gallo le cantara, si buen consejo tomara** – *Things would be very different.*
  Este refrán recomienda poner atención a los buenos consejos y las consecuencias que suelen derivarse de actuar sin tener en cuenta la opinión ajena.

■ **Ovejas bobas, por donde va una, van todas** – *Like lemmings to the sea.*

The Blind leading thre Blind.

Enseña que las personas de mala condición transmiten sus costumbres y sus vicios a aquellas que carecen de personalidad e iniciativa.

APUNTES:_____

_____

_____

P

- **Palabras al aire (al viento)** – *Hot air.*
  El marqués de Santillana cita este refrán en su recopilación titulada *Refranes que dicen las viejas tras el fuego*, y en él aconseja no hacer caso a las promesas fáciles ya que a menudo no se cumplen.

- **Pan con pan, comida de tontos** – *Variety is the spice of life.*
  Este refrán se refiere al hábito insulso y monótono que tiene ciertas personas de mezclar cosas afines o semejantes. Pero en algunos países de Latinoamérica lo han usado para censurar el matrimonio entre primos.

- **Para la muestra, un botón** – *You may know by a handful the whole sack.*
  Enseña este refrán que el todo está contenido en la parte, de modo que sólo con una pizca basta para entender la totalidad.

- **Para todo hay remedio, menos para la muerte** – *The only sure things are death and taxes.*
  Este refrán indica, que cualquier situación puede tener solución. Para lo único que no hay solución es para la muerte. Ésta es segura. Este refrán con alguna modificación se encuentra en *El Quixote* y en la novela *Cinco horas con Mario.*

- **Peleando las comadres se descubren las verdades** – *The truth will out.*
  Este refrán dice que cuando las personas se dejan llevar por las emociones y entran en disputas acaloradas sacan a relucir las faltas ocultas de sus mejores amigos. Hay varios refranes con la misma idea. El del marqués de Santillana reza: **Pelean los ladrones y descúbrense los hurtos**.

- **Perder por conocer no es perder** – *Good or bad, we learn from our experiences.*
  Este refrán enseña que aunque una experiencia sea mala, siempre es una buena experiencia puesto que ha enseñado una buena lección.

- **Perro de muchos amos** – *Jack of all trades.*
  Este refrán refiere a una persona que puede hacer todo o que tiene muchos talentos.

- **Perro ladrador, poco mordedor** – *His bark is worse than his bite.*
  Indica que aquellos que hablan demasiado, por lo general hacen muy poco.

- **Perro no come perro** – *There is honor among thieves.*
  Indica este refrán que las personas que son de la misma índole se respetan la una a la otra y no se van a causar daño entre ellas.

- **Perro que ladra no muerde** – *Barking dogs don´t bite.*
  Este refrán se dirige a las personas que presumen de bravas y corajudas o de las habitualmente fanfarronas.

- **Piano, piano se va lontano** – *Haste makes waste.*
  Little by little you'll go far.
  Es un refrán italiano que indica que haciendo las cosas despacio y calmadamente se llega lejos y mejor. En italiano, piano significa despacio o lento y lontano significa lejos.

- **Poderoso caballero es don dinero** – *Money talks.*
  Este refrán tomado de una famosa letrilla de Quevedo, explica la virtud tan poderosa que tiene el dinero. "Quién tiene dinero, tiene poder y todos obedecen".

- **Por el equipaje se conoce al pasajero** – *Fine feathers make fine birds.*
  Este refrán dice que un solo detalle es suficiente para valorar una cosa o a una persona. También indica que el principio o el inicio de algo permite deducir su final.

- **Por la boca muere el pez** – *Silence is golden.*
  Least said is soonest mended.
  Es un refrán de uso muy común. Delibes lo menciona en *Diario de un emigrante* y advierte que la persona indiscreta puede sufrir mucho daño y por lo tanto aconseja prudencia al hablar.

- **Por la hebra se saca el ovillo** – *Fine feathers make fine birds.*
  Este refrán tiene el mismo sentido que el anterior, **Por el equipaje se conoce al pasajero**, como también otro que reza: **Por la muestra se conoce el paño**. Es decir que con solo un detalle se puede valorar una cosa o una persona.

- **Por la plata baila el perro** – *There is nothing that money can't buy.*
  Que por el afán o por las necesidades de adquirir dinero, las personas están dispuestas a todo, sin escrúpulos ni miramientos.

- **Por ponerla Maria Ramos la pusimos la embarramos** – *Trying to do a goodwill and we mess things up.*
  Este refrán un poco moderno indica que por tratar de hacer una buena obra se hizo una no tan buena o que tuvo un mal resultado.

- **Por querer hacer una gracia hizo un gesto** – *Trying to do a goodwill and we mess things up.*
  Al igual que el refrán anterior, dice que por tratar de hacer buenas obras, a veces los resultados no son tan buenos.

- **Preguntando se va a Roma** – *Better to ask the way than to go astray.*
  Dice que se puede saber o encontrar algo con sólo preguntar y así no pasar por ignorante. Hay algunas variantes de este refrán.

- **Primero está la obligación que la devoción** – *Business before pleasure.*
  Según lo aconseja Perez Galdós en La capaña del Maestrazgo, se debe cumplir con los deberes primero y luego pensar en la diversión.

- **Prometer el oro y el moro** – *To promise the moon and stars.*
  Con esta expresión se alude a las promesas exageradas que se hacen para lograr u obligar a una persona a que haga algo.

- **Pueblo chiquito, infierno grande** – *Living in a small town can be hell.*

  Se refiere a las críticas, las incomodidades y a los rumores a que se hallan sujetas las personas que viven en villas y ciudades muy pequeñas.

  _____

  APUNTES:_____

  _____

  _____

Q

- **Quedó como mosca en leche** – *Unwelcome as a fly in the soup.*
Se usa para explicar que a veces las personas o las cosas están fuera de lugar o de su ambiente por la forma como se presentan o como se comportan.

- **Quien a buen árbol se arrima, buena sombra le cobija** – *It's always useful to have friends in high places.*
Este refrán se encuentra en el *Libro del caballero Zifar* y se refiere a las ventajas que logra la persona que tiene protección de alguien con poder.

- **Quien a hierro mata a hierro muere** – *He who lives by the sword shall die by the sword.*
Advierte que al que actúa mal, será tratado de la misma manera. En una canción moderna de Rubén Blades hay una variante de este refrán, dice: **Quien a hierro mata, a hierro termina**. Este proverbio se encuentra en el Evangelio de San Mateo 26:52.

- **Quien ama el peligro, en el perece** – *He who lives by the sword shall die by the sword.*
Hay algunas variantes de este refrán tales como **El que busca el peligro, en el perece** o **Quien busca el peligro, en el perece**.
Este refrán advierte que el mucho riesgo acaba trayendo malas o graves consecuencias. Se suele usar para amonestar a las personas muy osadas.

- **Quien con lobos anda a aullar aprende** – *If you lay down with dogs, you are going to get fleas.*
Enseña este refrán que al andar con malas compañías siempre se adquieren sus peores cualidades.

- **Quien da pan a perro ajeno, pierde el pan y pierde el perro y la amistad con el dueño** – *Never do business with family or friends.*
Este refrán recomienda no entrar en tratos y negocios con amigos, pues se corre el peligro de perderlo todo.

Quien mal anda, mal acaba – *Hard living leads to a bad end.*
Advierte que quien vive de mala manera y atado a las malas costumbres acaba víctima de estas.

Quien más tiene, más quiere – *The more you have, the more you want.*
Se refiere a la codicia de muchas personas ambiciosas que sin importar lo que tengan, todavía quieren más.

Quien nace para burro, muere rebuznando – *A leopard never changes its spots.*
Este refrán nos dice que todos tenemos ciertas características de personalidad que nunca cambiarán.

Querer es poder – *Where there is a will, there is a way.*
Este refrán afirma que la voluntad es la más fiel aliada de los deseos. Este proverbio vino del poeta Virgilio que dijo *"Possunt quia posse videntur"*.

APUNTES:_____

_____

_____

R

- **Remienda tu sayo y te durará un año, remiéndalo otra vez y te durará un mes** – *A stitch in time saves nine.*
  Aconseja cuidar restaurar las pertenencias de uso diario a tiempo para que duren y así no tener que hacer arreglos más graves en el futuro.

- **Respuesta mansa, la ira quebranta** – *A soft answer turns away wrath.*
  Una máxima latina dice **Quien domina la ira, vence a su mayor enemigo**. Este refrán aconseja hablar con suavidad y amabilidad y así aplacar la ira que pueda tener la otra persona.

APUNTES:

S

Sabe más el diablo por viejo que por diablo – *There is no substitute for experience.*
Destaca el valor de la experiencia como medio de conocimiento.

Salir de Guatemala y meterse en guatepeor – *Out of the frying pan, into the fire.*
Advierte que el deseo de evitar un mal puede conducir a otro peor.

Salga el alacrán de casa y pique donde picare – *Out of site, out of mind.*
Esta expresión indica que una vez que una persona que causa problemas se ha ido, ya no nos incumbe lo que haga o lo que le pueda ocurrir.

Sarna con gusto no pica – *It is up to him to live like that.*
Enseña que las molestias ocasionadas por asuntos placenteros sólo no incomodan pero pueden resultar agradables.

Se junta el hambre con las ganas de comer – *They are two of a kind.*
Este refrán se usa en una forma peyorativa para indicar que dos personas se compaginan muy bien. También se puede decir "tal para cual".

Se le subieron los humos a la cabeza – *The power went to his head.*
Se usa este refrán para indicar que una persona está actuando en una forma arrogante como resultado de un galardón que le han otorgado.

Ser harina de otro costal – *To be a horse of a different color.*
Este refrán indica que a una cosa no se aplica la misma actitud o consideración que a otra, tal vez parecida.

- **Si por allá llueve por aquí no escampa** – *When it rains, it pours.* Hace referencia a las calamidades colectivas. Advierte que a muchas personas les pueden ocurrir los mismos problemas.

- **Siempre se quiebra la soga por lo más delgado** – *A chain is only as strong as its weakest link.* Hace referencia a la supremacía del fuerte sobre el débil, el poderoso sobre el desvalido, el inteligente sobre el torpe y así continúa.

- **Sobre gustos no hay disgustos** – *Everyone has their own values.* Este refrán defiende la legitimidad y validez de todas las opiniones.

- **Sol que mucho madruga, poco dura** – *Soon ripe, soon rotten.* Da a entender este refrán que las cosas que se hacen a destiempo y con precipitación suelen concluir en fracaso.

- **Soldado advertido no muere en guerra** – *Better safe than sorry.* Este refrán exhorta a obrar con cautela cuando tenemos algún indicio de peligro. También advierte que si prestamos atención a las advertencias de otros, nada malo nos ocurrirá.

APUNTES:_____

_____

_____

T

- **Tantas manos en un plato huelen a caca de gato** – *Too many cooks spoil the broth.*
  Advierte que la intromisión de muchas personas en un asunto, seguramente lo echan a perder.

- **Tanto va el cántaro al agua que por fin se rompe** – *You shouldn't push your luck.*
  Este refrán se encuentra en *El Quixote* y advierte que el que frecuentemente se expone al peligro, termina al fin dañado. De este refrán hay muchas versiones antiguas.

- **Tirar la piedra y esconder la mano** – *To hit and run.*
  Se utiliza este refrán para denunciar a aquellos que después de cometer una fechoría no asumen su responsabilidad. El antiguo refrán decía Tirar la piedra y esconder la mano, hecho villano.

- **Tras de cotudo, con paperas** – *From bad to worse.*
  Se usa cuando a una persona le ocurren malos acontecimientos uno tras otro sin dar tregua.

APUNTES:_____

_____

_____

U

- **Una buena capa, todo lo tapa** – *Appearances are not always what they seem.*
Indica que una buena obra sirve, entre otras, para encubrir faltas y delitos.

- **Una cosa piensa el burro y otra el que lo está enjalmando** – *If you think that, you've another think coming.*
Por una parte este refrán trata de enseñar el modo de pensar entre el patrón y el subalterno. Por otra, dice que siempre hay personas que se aprovechan del trabajo de otros.

- **Una de cal y otra de arena** – *Six of one, and half a dozen of the other.*
Hace referencia a que lo mismo da una cosa que otra.

- **Un clavo saca otro clavo, o ambos se quedan adentro** – *One shoulder of mutton drives another one down.*
Este refrán tiene varias advertencias. Una enseña que la mejor manera de superar una adversidad es la aparición de una nueva. Por otro lado se usa para aconsejar que para acabar con un dolor, muchas veces es necesario emplear un remedio más doloroso y por último, es una forma de indicar venganza contra alguien que nos ha hecho el mal.

- **Un grano no hace granero, pero ayuda al compañero** - *Every little bit helps.*
Elogia la importancia del ahorro perseverante como vía de enriquecimiento y bienestar.

- **Uno tiene derecho a ser feo, pero bruto no** – *You have the right to be ugly, but not dumb.*
Esta expression indica que hay características que son innatas y no se pueden cambiar, pero hay otras que sí podemos cambiar y una de ellas es obrar con inteligencia y pensar bien las cosas.

Unos nacen con estrella y otros nacen estrellados – *Fortune smiles on some, but not on others.*
Este refrán da a entender la suerte con la que nacen las personas, indicando que ésta es predeterminada. Señala así la buena fortuna que siempre tienen algunas, mientras que hay otros que no importan cuanto traten, todo les resulta mal.

Unos tiene la fama y otros cardan la lana – *There are those that have and those that have not.*
Se emplea este refrán para advertir que a veces se inculpa a personas que no han hecho nada malo, mientras que se exculpa a los verdaderos responsables. También que se atribuye el mérito a quien no le corresponde.

APUNTES:_____

_____

_____

V

- **Vale más malo conocido, que bueno por conocer** – *Better the devil you know than the devil you don't.*
Este refrán dice que es mejor conservar aquello que se tiene, aunque no sea satisfactorio, que arriesgarse a salir engañado en el cambio.

- **Vemos la paja en el ojo ajeno, pero no la viga que tenemos en el propio** – *Look not for the speck in your brother's eye, but for the log in your own eye.*
Este refrán tiene su origen en el evangelio de San Mateo (7:3-5) que en forma diferente pregunta: *¿Cómo ves la paja en el ojo de tu hermano y no ves la viga en el tuyo?* Se refiere a la facilidad con que las personas no ven sus propios defectos, pero si notan el mínimo que puedan tener o en el que puedan incurrir las otras personas.

- **Ver y creer, dijo Santo Tomás** – *Seeing is believing.*
Es un proverbio que hace referencia a la falta de fe de Santo Tomas cuando supo que Cristo se les apareció a los apóstoles después de la resurrección. Enseña este refrán que no se debemos atenernos a las referencias verbales, sino que nos debemos confirmar la verdad con la vista.

- **Viejo desvergonzado hace al niño osado** – *There's no fool like an old fool.*
Aunque el equivalente no es exactamente el mismo, siempre tienen algo en común, ya que la persona desvergonzada hace que le pierdan el respeto.

- **Vino por lana y salió trasquilado** – *To be hoisted by one's own petard.*
Este refrán se refiere al incauto que piensa que va a sacra ganancia de algún asunto y todo lo que recibe son daños y pérdidas. También hace referencia a la persona que prepara una ofensa y sale ofendido.

APUNTES:_____

_____

_____

Y

- **Yerba mala, nunca muere** – *Only the good die young.*
Este refrán advierte que la gente de mala condición vive largos años, según la creencia supersticiosa.

APUNTES:_____

_____

_____

Z

- **Zamora no se ganó en una hora** – *Rome wasn't built in a day.*
  Recomienda paciencia ante toda obra de considerable envergadura.

- **Zapatero a tus zapatos** – *Mind your own business.*
  Este refrán recomienda no inmiscuirse en lo que no nos incumbe.
  Otras veces, para ahuyentar a la persona que incomoda en un
  trabajo con sus observaciones y comentarios.

APUNTES:_____

_____

_____

BIBLIOGRAPHY

Acuña, Luis Alberto. Refranero colombiano. Mil y un refranes. Bogotá, Colombia: Tres Culturas Editores., 1989.

Ammer, Christine. The American Heritage Dictionary of Idioms. Boston: Houghton Mifflin Company, 1997.

Azevedo, Milton M. Introducción a la Lingüística española. New Jersey: Prentice Hall, Inc., 1992.

Carbonell Basset, Delfín. Diccionario de Refranes, Proverbios, Dichos y Adagios. Barcelona, España: Ediciones del Serbal, 1996.

Casado Conde, María Leonisa. Se dice pronto. Madrid, España: Ediciones Internacionales Universitarias, S.A., 2002.

Fernández, Mauro. Diccionario de refranes. España: Gráficas Marte, 1994.

Foster, David William. Literatura española, una antología. New York & London: Garland Publishing, Inc., 1995.

Funk, Charles Earle, Heavens To Betsy! & Other Curious Sayings. New York: Harper Collins Publishers Inc., 1955.

González, Rosean Dueñas, Victoria E. Vásquez, Holly Mikkelson. Fundamentals of Court Interpretation: Theory, Policy and Practice. Durham, NC., Caroline Academic Press, 1991.

Junceda, Luis. Diccionario de refranes. Madrid: Editorial Espasa Calpe, S.A., 1998.

Korach, Myron, and John B. Mordock. Common Phrases and Where they Come From. Guilford, CT: The Lyons Press, 2002.

Maldonado, Felipe C.R.. Refranero clásico español y otros dichos populares. España: Taurus Ediciones, S.A., 1974.

Mertvago, Peter, Dictionary of 1000 Proverbs. New York: Hippocrene Books, Inc., 1996.

Nelson & Sons, Thomas. The Holy Bible. Revised Standard Version. New

York: Thomas Nelson & Sons, Limited, 1953.

Pérez, Ángeles, Rafael Sala, Manuel Santamaría. <u>Cassell's Contemporary Spanish</u>. New York, NY: Macmillan Publishing Company, 1993.

CiberTextos Interactivos. <u>La Celestina, Refranes y Locuciones</u>. April 2002.
http://aaswebsv.aas.duke.edu/celestina.html.

Rogers, James. <u>The Dictionary of Clichés</u>. New York, NY.: Wings Books, 1985.

Rorty, Amélie Oksenberg. <u>The Many Faces of Evil</u>: London and New York, Routledge, 2001.

Samper Pizano, Daniel. "Nuevos refranes para nuevos manes." <u>Carrusel</u> January 30, 2003. El Tiempo, Bogotá, Colombia. 30 January, 2003.
http://eltiempo.terra.com.co/proyectos/humor/nevosrefranesparanue.

INDEX
ENGLISH TO SPANISH

A

B

C

D

E

F

G

H

I

J

K

L

M

N

O

P

R

S

T

U

V

W

Y

ÍNDICE
ESPAÑOL A INGLÉS

A

B

C

D

E

G

H

I

L

M

N

O

P

Q

R

S

T

U

V

Y

Z